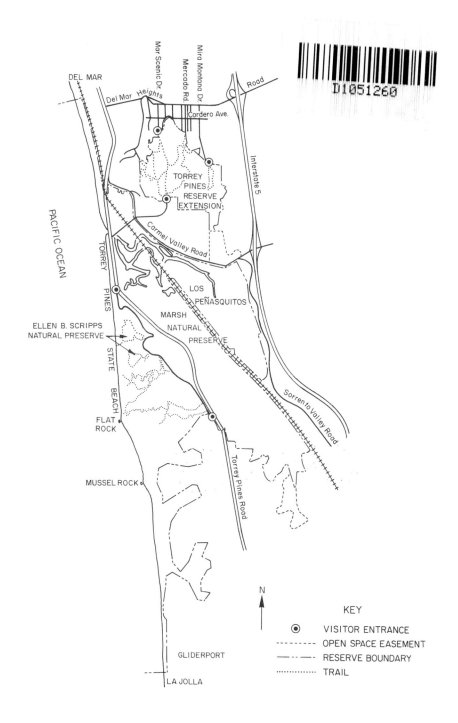

Map of the Torrey Pines State Reserve and Extension, showing Los Peñasquitos Marsh Natural Preserve and the Ellen B. Scripps Natural Preserve with access points and trails.

1

This booklet is published by the TORREY PINES ASSOCIATION to record the history, to describe the flora and fauna and to give an account of the geological and archaeological significance of the area comprising TORREY PINES STATE RESERVE. It is hoped to create a desire for the preservation of the natural beauty of this unique area.

The text has been approved by the Department of Parks and Recreation, State of California. The counselors of the Torrey Pines Association are grateful to those who have given time and effort to the preparation of this publication.

Special acknowledgment is due to Mrs. Nackey S. Meanley and to the Francis P. Shepard Foundation, whose generosity made the first edition possible.

TORREY PINES STATE RESERVE

A SCIENTIFIC RESERVE OF THE
DEPARTMENT OF PARKS AND RECREATION
STATE OF CALIFORNIA

Dedicated by the State of California
TO THE PRESERVATION
OF THE RARE TORREY PINE
AND ITS ENVIRONMENT

Edited by
CARL L. HUBBS AND THOMAS W. WHITAKER
FREDA M. H. REID: *THIRD EDITION*

Published by
THE TORREY PINES ASSOCIATION
LA JOLLA, CALIFORNIA
September, 1964
Second Edition, April, 1972
Third Edition, June, 1991

3

ISBN 0-9629917-0-8
Library of Congress Catalog Number 91-65594

A Wind-Blown Torrey Pine

Guy L. Fleming

DEDICATION*

The name of Guy L. Fleming will always be closely associated with Torrey Pines State Reserve. Naturalist, conservationist, and park administrator, Guy for many years made this beautiful spot, with its sweeping views of the Pacific and its colony of unique picturesque pines, a point of departure for his many adventures. His activities contributed richly to the preservation of the native landscape of California.

It was here, in a home that he and his artist wife, Margaret, had designed and Guy had largely built with his own hands, that he superintended the protection of the Torrey Pines. This responsibility was given to him by Miss Ellen Browning Scripps in recognition of the fact that Guy had largely inspired the creation of the reservation.

It was from here that he conceived and carried out projects like the Anza-Borrego Desert State Park, Mt. San Jacinto and Mt. Palomar, the Silver Strand and other beach parks in Southern California, and the restoration of historic sites like La Purisima Mission and Pio Pico Mansion.

It was from his headquarters in Torrey Pines Reserve that, as District Superintendent, he administered a steadily-growing assemblage of seacoast, mountain and desert parks, together with historic sites, in the southern district of the California State Park System.

During the '30's under the Civilian Conservation Corps, the newly-formed California State Park System was developed with Federal funds. It was fortunate indeed that Guy was there to superintend this work in some of the most important and perishable state parks. He was a practical construction man, but his motto was "restraint."

Guy was a rare combination of sensitivity and strength. It was my privilege to be his comrade-in-arms in the many battles to preserve the varied beauty and significance of the California landscape. He never faltered. He never compromised in his recommendations. He was indefatigable, and accomplished many formidable tasks because he had the advantage of not knowing that "it couldn't be done." The California State Park System bears his imprint at many places, but mostly particularly at Torrey Pines State Reserve.

Newton B. Drury
1964

*The officers and members of the Torrey Pines Association take pleasure in dedicating this booklet to Guy L. Fleming, protector of the Torrey Pines and founder of the Association. For the preservation of the Reserve in a nearly natural state, we are deeply indebted to the perseverance of Mr. Fleming from 1921 until the time of his death in 1960. Following in the footsteps of Mr. Fleming, Dr. John A. Comstock during the 1960's worked hard and effectively for the preservation of the Reserve when it was menaced by commercial interests. Mr. Newton B. Drury, distinguished conservationist, and good friend of Mr. Fleming, prepared the dedication.

CONTRIBUTORS

ORIGINAL CONTRIBUTORS

Michael D. Atkins

John S. Bradshaw

John A. Comstock*

Joseph F. Copp

E. Yale Dawson*

Newton B. Drury*

Margaret E. Fleming*

Sam Hinton

Carl L. Hubbs*

Douglas L. Inman

Ruth Inman*

Monte N. Kirven

Laurence M. Klauber*

James R. Moriarty

Peta Mudie

Charles E. Nordstrom

A. John Sloan

Larned L. Tuttle

Thomas W. Whitaker

Helen Witham*

*deceased

1991 EDITION CONTRIBUTORS

Harriet Allen

R. Mitchel Beauchamp

William Brothers

Maurie M. Brown

Fred J. Crowe

Ross E. Dingman

Marion Dixon

Susan R. Green

Philip Kern

David King

Margaret D. Knight

Jessie LaGrange

Patricia Masters

Barbara C. Moore

Freda M. H. Reid

Richard H. Rosenblatt

John S. Shelton

Marie A. Simovich

Joan G. Stewart

Robert S. Wohl

With special thanks to Harriet Allen whose wide knowledge of the Reserve and its history were invaluable. Also to Mitchel Beauchamp (of Pacific Southwest Biological Services) for considerable technical assistance.

Etchings and drawings by MARGARET EDDY FLEMING
Photographs by SUSAN R. GREEN

TABLE OF CONTENTS

HISTORY OF TORREY PINES STATE RESERVE

The Torrey Pine, *Pinus torreyana* Parry, is the rarest American pine tree and the third rarest pine in the world. This species is indigenous to two small areas: Del Mar and Torrey Pines State Reserve, and Santa Rosa Island, one of the Channel Islands southwest of Santa Barbara. The Torrey Pine bears a cluster of five long, stout needle-like leaves encased in a basal sheath. The cones are large and woody, and the seeds large, thick-shelled and edible. In its native habitat it grows into wind-sculpted and picturesque forms of great beauty.

Torrey Pines State Reserve, between the northern limits of the City of San Diego and the City of Del Mar, is a remarkable natural monument, an outdoor museum provided by nature. During the hundreds of thousands of years involved in shaping the Torrey Pines Mesa great changes in the climate and landscape occurred, profoundly altering the character of the fauna and flora. As a result, the Torrey Pines have gradually been restricted in area. They have made their last stand among the rugged canyons, clinging to the painted cliffs of this unusual natural region and on Santa Rosa Island.

Today, many of the trees are found battling for their existence on the infertile, stony soil of their ancestors. Dwarfed, gnarled, twisted, and beaten almost to the ground, they send their roots spreading in every direction seeking food and water and a stronger foothold. They are marvelous examples of the tenacity of plant life and of adaptation to a rugged environment.

The early Spanish navigators were impressed by the fact that trees were not common along the coast of Southern California and gave to the location of these pines the name "Punta de los Arboles" (Point of Trees). Likewise, the "Coast Pilot" of 1889 states:

> "Pine Hill—one mile south of Del Mar and six miles northward from Point La Jolla. There is a hillock of 346 feet elevation sparsely covered with pines. As this is the only pine covered hillock for miles along the coastline, it is an important landmark to vessels that are running close along shore in foggy weather."

This tree was early recognized as a remarkable botanical relic with a limited number of living representatives. For these reasons conservation-minded citizens commenced as early as 1850 to give some thought to measures that would save and protect this rare species for the enjoyment and instruction of future generations. In March 1883, Dr. C. C. Parry, who described the Torrey

Figure 1—*An isolated Torrey Pine tree.*

Pine botanically, revisited the area and reported to the San Diego Society of Natural History that the trees were in danger of being exterminated. He challenged San Diego to acquire these lands:

> "to secure the growth from threatened extermination. . . and to dedicate this spot of ground forever to the cause of scientific instruction and recreation."

In March 1899, George W. Marston and others induced the City of San Diego to set aside its own adjacent lands containing canyons and trees as the original reserve for the Torrey Pines. It remained, however, for Miss Ellen B. Scripps, citizen and philanthropist of La Jolla, to purchase and protect Torrey Pines Point with its unsurpassed groves of Torrey Pines. It was her idea to preserve this precious heritage, with its unique association of trees and shrubs, for the enjoyment of present and future generations.

Miss Scripps' vision for preserving the Torrey Pines was translated into action by Guy L. Fleming. Fleming was a well-known naturalist, and an authority on the native trees and shrubs of Southern California, with many years of experience in the California State Park Service. In 1950 he founded the Torrey Pines Association, an organization dedicated to the preservation of the unique Torrey Pines. Under the sponsorship of the Torrey Pines Association, combined with the lively interest of Californians and particularly of San Diegans and La Jollans, the Torrey Pines Reserve was transferred by the City of San Diego to the State of California in 1959. Thus it became one of the chain of State beaches and parks that includes some of the most outstanding and scenic locations in California.

The following is the story of the discovery of the Torrey Pine and the history of Torrey Pines State Reserve, compiled from the records of Guy L. Fleming.

The unique maritime pine found growing at the northern limits of the city of San Diego was not recognized as an unusual tree by the early Spanish explorers or the Mexican colonists. The first Americans to visit the region called the trees the Soledad (solitary) Pines because they grew on the seaward slopes of both sides of the entrance to Soledad Valley (now called Sorrento Valley).

The pine was recognized as a new species in the spring of 1850 (the year the state was admitted to the Union) by Dr. C. C. Parry, official botanist of the U.S.-Mexican Boundary Survey. He named this tree *Pinus torreyana* Parry, in honor of his friend and instructor, Dr. John Torrey of Columbia University, one of the foremost American botanists of that period. These pine groves were so remote from the little village of San Diego in 1850 to 1880 that there was no mention of the trees in the public press until Parry returned to San Diego and the Torrey Pines area early in 1883.

At a meeting of the San Diego Society of Natural History in March 1883, Parry presented an historical account of the discovery of *Pinus torreyana*. In describing the extent of the pine groves he states:

> "The bulk of the tree growth is here confined to a series of high broken cliffs and deeply indented ravines on the bold headlands overlooking the sea south of Soledad Valley and within the corporate limits of the town of San Diego. Within a radius of not more than half a mile, this singular species may be seen at its best advantage, clinging to the face of crumbling yellowish sandstone or shooting up in more graceful forms its scant foliage in the shelter of deep ravines bathed with frequent sea fog."

Dr. Parry concluded his remarks with this stimulating suggestion:

> "Why should not San Diego, within whose corporate limits this struggling remnant of a past age finds a last lingering resting place, secure from threatened extermination this remarkable and unique Pacific Coast production so singularly confined within its boundaries; dedicating this spot of ground forever to the cause of scientific instruction and recreation, where wiser generations than ours may sit beneath its ampler shade, and listening to the same musical waves, thank us for sparing this tree? And finally why is not the San Diego Society of Natural History the suitable body to recommend such action?"

That the members of the San Diego Society of Natural History did respond to this plea is evident from the following "warning" posted by the Board of Supervisors in the Torrey Pines area and in public places in 1885.

WARNING
$100 REWARD!

> At a regular meeting of the Board of Supervisors of San Diego County, held July 11th, 1885, it was ordered that a reward of $100 be paid by said Board for the detection and conviction of any person guilty of removing, cutting, or otherwise destroying any of the Torrey Pines (known as *Pinus torreyana*) now growing in Soledad and vicinity.—By order of the Board of Supervisors.—J. M. DODGE, Clerk.

13

In 1887 and 1888 the newly created California State Board of Forestry assigned a botanist, Mr. J. G. Lemmon of San Bernardino, to make a study of the pine trees of California. Lemmon made his headquarters at Del Mar, while investigating the pines of San Diego County. He devoted considerable time to a study of the Torrey Pine. The following quotation from his report is of interest.

> "Young trees were noted in several localities, some just struggling above the grass and flowers. Spade holes here and there show that trees have been lately removed for cultivation; also a few stumps are seen but generally north and south of Soledad Valley the groves seem to have been allowed to remain unmolested. Notwithstanding this happily untouched condition of these trees, with the influx of immigration this lovely seaside area is destined to receive a large population, and then these trees will be menaced with extermination at the hands of men, unless steps are taken to protect them, as suggested in the closing paragraph of Dr. Parry's paper, or better they should be preserved by the State of California through the efforts of proper legislation. . ."

In June of 1888 Mr. T. S. Brandegee, an enthusiastic and capable botanist, made the first recorded botanical survey of Santa Rosa Island. On the northeast shore of the island, Brandegee discovered a small grove of Torrey Pine trees. The discovery of this rare pine on Santa Rosa Island, 175 miles north and west of the mainland groves, suggests that some time before the Channel Islands were isolated from the mainland, the ancestors of the Torrey Pine may have formed an extensive forest along the former coastline of Southern California.

About 1890 the Pueblo lands north of Old Town, and including the Torrey Pine lands at the northern limits of San Diego, were leased for cattle and sheep grazing. Pines, manzanita, and other shrubs were cut and hauled away for fuel, and fires often swept over the tract. In 1895 Miss Belle Angier carried out a botanical assignment in the Torrey Pines area for Dr. Charles Sprague Sargent, Director of the Arnold Arboretum, Harvard University. Impressed by the threatened extermination of the Torrey Pine groves, she appealed to George Marston, Daniel Cleveland and other active members of the San Diego Society of Natural History to petition the City Council to take specific action to assure their preservation.

On August 10, 1899, the Common Council of San Diego passed an ordinance setting aside 369 acres in Pueblo Lots 1332, 1333, 1336, and 1337 as a public park. The ordinance declared that "the same shall forever be held in trust by the municipal authorities as a free and public park." Further, it states, "that there is growing upon said lands certain rare and valuable trees of the variety known as *Pinus torreyana*, and that it is the wish and desire of the said City of San Diego to preserve these trees."

The finest groves of Torrey Pines and associated flora, and some of the most picturesquely carved cliffs and canyons, lie to the north of the original Torrey Pines Park, in Pueblo Lots 1338 and 1339. These Pueblo Lots were sold to private interests by the City of San Diego in about 1870. Soon after 1900 there was a plan to subdivide or otherwise commercialize these lots. George Marston and E. W. Scripps interested Miss Ellen B. Scripps in acquiring these privately-owned lots. In June 1908 she purchased Pueblo Lot 1338, and later in June 1911, she also purchased a portion of Pueblo Lot 1339. This was followed by the acquisition in August 1912, of an additional portion of the Pueblo Lot 1339. The latter purchase included all the trees lying between the old Torrey Pines Grade and the Santa Fe Railway.

In June 1916, Fleming and Ralph Sumner, representing the San Diego Society of Natural History and the San Diego Floral Association, made a two day visit to the Torrey Pines area to conduct botanical studies. They were alarmed by fire scars in all parts of the pine area, and by the evidence of uncontrolled camping and picnicking, indicating these rare trees were being used for firewood. Their reports resulted in stimulating a strong movement in San Diego to preserve the Torrey Pines and their unusual environment from further threat.

Miss Scripps, became the patroness of the movement to save the Torrey Pines. In June 1921, with the concurrence of the City Park Commission,she appointed Fleming as Custodian of the lands purchased for park purposes and the City-owned lands upon which Torrey Pines were growing. The entire area was designated a reservation and named Torrey Pines Reserve.

In the summer of 1922, Miss Scripps financed the construction of Torrey Pines Lodge. It was opened to the public in February, 1923. This one-story adobe structure, on the cliffs overlooking the scenic Painted Gorge, was built upon the City-owned portion of Torrey Pines Reserve. It was a liberal gift from Miss Scripps to the people of San Diego.

In 1924 the City Park Commission, in cooperation with interested civic groups, prevailed upon the City Council to enact an ordinance adding other pueblo lands to the Torrey Pines Reserve. At that time the area included nearly 1,000 acres of rugged cliffs and canyons, rolling mesa lands, and all of Los Peñasquitos Lagoon lying west of the Santa Fe Railway. It had a sea frontage of three miles, extending from the Del Mar-San Diego boundary at the Torrey

Pines overhead crossing southward to and including Indian Canyon, beyond the Flat (Bathtub) Rock.

On June 5, 1956, a special city election was held at which the proposition "to convey portions of Torrey Pines Park, not to exceed 1000 acres to the State of California for park purposes" was passed by well over two-thirds majority of the electorate. On May 7, 1959, title was vested in the State of California. The area is now classified as a Scientific Reserve and is operated by the Department of Parks and Recreation, State of California. Within the Reserve there are two Preserves with more restrictive uses: the Ellen B. Scripps Natural Preserve and the Los Peñasquitos Marsh Natural Preserve.

Other events could be related that are equally pertinent to the active and continuous interest manifested by many persons and organizations in assuring the preservation of the rare Torrey Pines in their original and unique setting. But it is proper here to call attention to Miss Scripps' prediction "that the time will come when not only the scenic beauty but also the educational and recreational values of the Torrey Pines Reserve will be appreciated."

As of 1990, the entire State Reserve exceeded 1,500 acres with approximately 5,500 trees growing in their native mainland habitat.

Figure 2—*Many of the pines are gnarled and twisted from age-long battles against wind and drought. Old, dead trees are allowed to remain in their natural habitat.*

BRIEF CHRONOLOGY OF TORREY PINES
STATE RESERVE

Prior to 1850	The Torrey Pine trees were called Soledad Pines; their location was known as "Punta de los Arboles" and later as "Pine Hill."
1850	The pines were described as a new species, *Pinus torreyana*, by Dr. C. C. Parry, botanist for the U.S.-Mexican Boundary Survey.
1883	Parry revisited the area and made a comprehensive report to the San Diego Society of Natural History.
1885	The Board of Supervisors, San Diego County, posted a reward of $100 for apprehension of anyone despoiling Torrey Pine trees.
1888	J. G. Lemmon's report to the State Board of Forestry suggested protection of the trees by appropriate legislation. T. S. Brandegee discovered a stand of Torrey Pines on Santa Rosa Island.
1890	Pueblo lands including the site of the future Torrey Pines State Reserve leased for cattle and sheep grazing.
1895	Miss Belle Angier, a local botanical collector, urged local conservation groups to support legislative action for the protection and preservation of the trees.
1899	The Common Council of San Diego designated 369 acres in the area as a public park, to be known as the TORREY PINES PARK.
1901-02	Wagon roads were extended into the park.
1908-12	Miss Ellen Browning Scripps acquired several groves of Torrey Pines.
1915	The Torrey Pines Grade and coastal road was completed.
1916	Guy L. Fleming and Ralph Sumner reported that the trees were being steadily destroyed for firewood.
1921	Fleming was appointed custodian of Torrey Pines Park, by Miss Scripps and the San Diego City Board of Park Commissioners. The entire area was renamed the TORREY PINES RESERVE. Miss Scripps engaged landscape architect, Ralph Cornell, to recommend plans for protecting as well as developing the new reserve.
1922	Miss Scripps financed the construction of the Torrey Pines Lodge completed in 1923.
1924	The Torrey Pines Reserve was enlarged by the City Council to approximately 1,000 acres. Coast Highway 101 was constructed over Torrey Pines Hill.

1927	The Guy L. Fleming residence was completed. The state legislature authorized the establishment of the California Park Commission and the Division of Parks.
1930	An expanded Highway 101 approved along the east side of the reserve as a compromise to a cliff route along the ocean.
1950	The Torrey Pines Association was incorporated.
1952	The City of San Diego turned over the Torrey Pines Beach to the State Park system.
1956	By a vote of the electorate of the City of San Diego, ownership of the Reserve lands, not to exceed 1,000 acres, was conveyed to the State of California. A vote also appropriated about 100 acres from the south end of the Reserve for a golf course.
1959	The City of San Diego conveyed title for the Reserve to the State Park system. The area where the Torrey Pines were located was referred to as a "Scientific Reserve."
1964	A large State Bond Issue was approved by the voters. Citizens living among Torrey Pines north of the Lagoon launched a campaign to apply for Bond money to add two groves to the State Reserve. These were located north and south of Del Mar Heights Road almost joining the San Dieguito and Los Peñasquitos lagoons. These groves would have added about 260 acres and 3,000 trees to the Reserve. An "Extension Campaign" was established.
1965	The Torrey Pines Association, other organizations and schools joined the "Extension Campaign."
1966	The State Park Commission recommended in principle the acquisition of the Extension parcels. The Guy L. Fleming Trail was dedicated, May 27.
1967	The State of California Legislature endorsed the Park Commission's action and allocated $900,000 in bond money to be expended, on a matching basis, for the acquisition of lands for the Torrey Pines Extension.
1970	Two subunits of the Reserve were reclassified as Preserves: Los Peñasquitos Marsh Natural Preserve (lands and waters lying below 20 feet elevation) and the Torrey Pines Natural Preserve. The latter was renamed the Ellen B. Scripps Natural Preserve in March, 1983.
1971	The Daughters of the American Revolution Trail and Bench were dedicated in the Extension area on November 16, 1971. The beach subunit, lying below 5 feet elevation, was reclassified from State Reserve to State Beach.

1974	The official Extension Campaign was closed with the addition of 168 acres and approximately 1,500 trees. Two celebrations were held: The Torrey Pines Association on February 14, and the official state ceremony on August 20 at Del Mar School.
1975	Torrey Pines Docent Society was established.
1978	The Torrey Pines State Reserve was dedicated as a National Natural Landmark, a designation of the Department of the Interior.
1978-81	The Youth Conservation Corps created new trails, and renovated old ones in the Broken Hills, Beach and Razor Point areas.
1980	The Guy L. Fleming residence was saved from demolition and renovated by funds provided by the Torrey Pines Association for use as a residence for park personnel.
1982	The Los Peñasquitos Foundation was established.
1983	The General Plan for Torrey Pines State Beach was approved.
1984	The General Plan for Torrey Pines State Reserve was approved with provisions for overnight camping at the north parking lot.
1987-88	Rehabilitation of the Ellen B. Scripps Lodge was completed.
1988	Additional trail renovation in the Beach and Razor Point areas was done by the state.
1980-89	Additions to the Reserve and Lagoon were achieved through Park Bond monies, easements and Los Peñasquitos Lagoon Foundation funds. Parcels included the Beau Soleil, Lance Allworth, San Diego Gas & Electric Company and Portofino Extension properties.
1990	Renovation of the Reserve entrance, paving of the south parking lot and modernization of facilities was authorized and completed in 1991.

HISTORY OF TORREY PINES STATE
RESERVE EXTENSION

The history of the Torrey Pines State Reserve Extension lacks the romantic flavor that the passage of time has lent to the history of the original Torrey Pines State Reserve. A great conservation battle was won, in the face of overwhelming odds, by citizens devoted to the purpose of preserving the last unprotected groves of Torrey Pines and to saving those vestiges of our urban environment that still retain their natural beauty and unique resources. It took approximately 30 years (from 1883 to 1912) to assure the protection of the Torrey Pines in the original Reserve area, during an age of philanthropists and slow growth in the area. Between 1964 and 1970, this earlier conservation effort was recapitulated within 6 years, during the struggle to acquire the Extension area against a background of soaring land prices and a booming housing industry. It is the story of this remarkable modern-day conservation achievement that deserves a special chapter in the history of the Torrey Pines State Reserve.

The Torrey Pines State Reserve Extension, located approximately one mile north of the original Torrey Pines State Reserve, is an area of rugged ridge and canyon topography, clothed by several magnificent groves of Torrey Pines and a wide variety of native shrubs. Geologically and ecologically, the Extension is an integral part of the Torrey Pines State Reserve as it comprises a northward extension of the bluffs south of Los Peñasquitos Valley. However, the northern extension area is not just a mirror image of the southern portion of the Reserve: its topography and vegetation is very distinctive.

The geology of the Extension is characterized by two major upland blocks of eroded ridges and ravines that frame a broad central valley of more gentle relief, forming a vast natural amphitheater. The western bluff area is dominated by smooth, wind-carved outcroppings of white sandstone; in contrast, the eastern uplands are characterized by razor-like ridges and precipitous cliffs which are capped by a rust-colored layer of resistant, iron-bearing sedimentary rock. From these eastern cliffs, a series of rounded, white ridges undulate down toward the central lowland. This central valley is bisected by a sandy wash in which a small stream flows during early spring. Unfortunately, the natural beauty of this valley has been marred by a fire that swept through the area in 1962 and by a 10-foot-deep erosion gully which developed following the removal of the protective brush cover in 1964. These scars serve as a reminder of the fragile nature of the Torrey Pines area and of the fact that natural geological and ecological changes are usually recorded in centuries and aeons, while man-made changes, many of them inadvertently caused, often produce major alterations in geology and ecology within months or years.

From a botanical viewpoint, the Extension is interesting because of the presence of several kinds of native plants absent from the main Reserve area. Most conspicuous are the Coastal Blue Lilac, which covers part of the upland mesa in pale blue lace during early spring, and the spectacular Scarlet Larkspur, the red trumpets of which may be seen on the slopes of the central valley in late spring. In addition to those unique plants, several fairly large shrubs, notably the Tree Poppy, the Bush Mallow, the Eastwood Manzanita, and the Jojoba or Goatnut, are much more abundant in the Extension than in the southern park area. On the other hand, several of the low-growing plants that clothe the exposed maritime bluffs of the main Torrey Pines State Reserve are not present in the Extension because of the absence of this type of habitat.

Most of the trees in the Extension are in fine condition and show vigorous growth in comparison with many of the trees on the wind-swept bluffs of the southern park. The trees on these dry, sandy, southern cliffs have suffered from the invasion of bark beetles and from centuries of exposure to strong winds and salt-laden air. In contrast, the more sheltered inland habitat of the Extension area has provided the northern Torrey Pines with more favorable growing conditions, as may be witnessed by the presence of a relatively large number of healthy young trees.

Concern over the vulnerability of the Torrey Pines in the original Reserve to beetle depredation and brush fires prompted the effort to extend the boundaries of the Reserve in order to protect the fine trees on the northern bluffs. Furthermore, the rapid growth of the resident and tourist population along the coast of San Diego County was beginning to cause problems of overuse in the fragile, easily-eroded habitat of the Reserve. Perhaps the most compelling factor leading to the effort to extend the Reserve boundaries, however, was the encroachment of housing developments on the mesa just beyond the northern groves of Torrey Pines. Thus, while the incorporation into the Reserve of the Torrey Pines on the northern bluffs had long been the dream of local conservationists, it was not until these trees were physically threatened with removal that the battle for their preservation finally began.

The story of how the movement to protect these trees started with a small group of local conservationists and evolved into a nationwide fund-raising effort is a remarkable example of cooperative citizen action. It began in November 1964, when Robert Bates and his wife, both dedicated

Figure 3—*Beginning of the Guy L. Fleming Trail: chaparral and eroded sandstone cliffs.*

22

conservationists and far-sighted citizens, were walking among the Torrey Pine groves behind their home and discovered that fine mature Torrey Pines were being razed to the ground by bulldozers during the construction of a new road. Bates immediately alerted the Superintendent of the Torrey Pines State Reserve, the Torrey Pines Association, the Sierra Club, and Citizens Coordinate, a local concern dedicated to the preservation of environmental quality in the San Diego area. Shortly thereafter, the Citizens Committee for Extension of Torrey Pines Reserve was organized and formulated plans for the northward expansion of the State Reserve and published a booklet outlining the need for the Extension.

As originally conceived by the committee, the Extension boundaries would have encompassed an area of 260 acres, extending from the northeast shore of Los Peñasquitos Lagoon across the northern bluffs to include a beautiful pine-covered valley on the north side of the mesa behind Del Mar.

The publication of the booklet led to the successful adoption, in May 1965, of a Resolution by the State Assembly directing the California Resources Agency to study the Extension proposal. Later that year, however, the first disappointment was suffered when the State Parks Commission turned down the proposal on the grounds that sufficient Torrey Pines were already protected within the existing Reserve. Through the continued effort of the Committee members, however, resolutions of support for the proposed Extension were obtained from many citizen organizations, from city officials, and from all local State legislators. An important contribution was also made at this stage by the Ellen B. Scripps Foundation which provided the nucleus of the Torrey Pines campaign fund and the tangible evidence that citizens of the San Diego area were serious about acquiring the proposed Extension.

The first major success came in January 1966 when the State Parks Commission, after studying the Extension proposal, recommended that one and a half million dollars in State Park bond funds be allocated to the Extension project, providing that additional funds be made available from private or other sources to complete the necessary funding. At the same time, however, a blow was dealt to the hopeful conservationists when it was found that the boundaries of the proposed Extension had been shrunk to include only 214 of the original 260 acres and that the plans now excluded the northernmost valley behind Del Mar as well as the provision for the youth-group camping facilities.

Any disappointment generated by these changes, however, was overshadowed by the events that followed in the 1966 legislative session when northern political officials successfully sought to wrestle the appropriation of state funds away from Southern California. After the preliminary allocation of five million dollars for the joint acquisition of the Torrey Pines Extension and Old Town Park in San Diego, a series of budget squeezes followed that finally culminated in the reduction of the allotted Old Town funds and the complete elimination of all budgeted funds for the proposed Extension.

This slashing of funds for the acquisition of the Extension meant that, after the tremendous effort of the 1965-66 publicity campaign, the Citizens Committee was once again faced with the task of enlisting public and legislative support for the Extension plan. Discouraged, yet still determined, they regrouped in the fall of 1966 to form the Council for Extension of Torrey Pines State Reserve. This Council now represented the determination of the Torrey Pines Association, the Sierra Club, the San Diego Society of Natural History and the Torrey Pines Wildlife Association to save the endangered pines. A multi-phase program was launched in an attempt to make legislators and the general public aware of the scenic and wildlife resources in the proposed Extension. This publicity effort culminated in February 1967, with a "Save the Torrey Pines Week" and the publication of a sixteen-page tabloid on the Torrey Pines State Reserve, which subsequently earned several literary awards and letters of congratulation from the White House and the Secretary of the Interior, Stewart Udall.

This second major effort to save the Pines was rewarded in April 1967, when the State approved the allocation of approximately one million dollars in Park Bond funds to finance the Extension proposal. This turned out to be a bitter-sweet victory for the conservationists, however, when it was made clear that these funds were to be matched by money raised from sources other than the State. Furthermore, it became apparent that for the first time in the history of the California State Parks, the money for a State Park would have to be raised by citizens without the facilitation of county or city bonds. The Torrey Pines Extension Council now found itself faced with the awesome task of somehow raising almost $900,000 before the end of the legislative session in 1970 and of accomplishing this effort by asking citizens to reach into their pockets and match, dollar for dollar, the amount that they had already committed to the park in state bonds.

The prospect of raising this amount of money to save a few thousand trees at first seemed little short of overwhelming. Since the Torrey Pines Extension Council did not have the organizational status to hold funds, it was dissolved and the Torrey Pines Association, which already held the nucleus of a fund for the acquisition of the Extension, took over the campaign. Led by Margaret Fleming and Thomas W. Whitaker, a two-pronged effort was launched by this conservation group: firstly, landowners in the Extension area were urged to contribute land (some of it valued as high as $30,000 per acre) and substantial monetary gifts were sought from a relatively small number of people and foundations; secondly, a monumental effort was made to awaken public awareness of the beauty and uniqueness of the Torrey Pines area. Later, in

25

1969, Edward T. Butler, a prominent San Diego attorney, assumed the chairmanship of the funding drive which became known as the Torrey Pines Extension Campaign.

The public response to this appeal to save the pines was fantastic. Local and national news media gave the concern generous coverage; social, civic and church groups responded with donations and fund-raising activities; bake-sales were held and cartons of Torrey Pine seedlings were sold; trees and trails in the proposed Extension were "bought" by individuals who firmly believed in the future of the Reserve. Perhaps the most impressive response came from the younger citizens: elementary school children sold homemade articles, high school students held dances, slave days and chariot races, and college students sold Torrey Pines Christmas cards and organized fund-raising walks. There was never any question about the monetary value of Torrey Pine trees; it was simply a matter of realizing that a rare and beautiful area had to be saved from the encroachment of urban destruction.

By the spring of 1970 well over 3,000 persons had contributed financially to the Extension campaign and the plight of the groves of Pines on the wind-carved bluffs near Del Mar was widely known. About $700,000 in donations and pledges had been secured, including land in the Extension. Finally, in the summer of 1970, the State Legislature confirmed the allocation of $900,000 in Park Bonds for the appropriation of the Reserve Extension and released the money for the purchase of the first parcel of land.

With the acquisition of the first 73 acres of the Torrey Pines Extension in August 1970, the six-year dream finally began to become a reality. However, the ambitious program had been scaled down to 197 acres. The beautiful Crest Canyon Grove proved beyond the fiscal possibility and presented severe management problems. Unwilling sellers and developers who "got in under the wire" further reduced the potential acquisition of the whole Extension area.

When the official campaign ended in 1974, 168 acres had been acquired for the Reserve. A magnificent accomplishment for a grass-roots project! Thousands of citizens had contributed time and financial resources for the acquisition of this natural monument. The beautiful Extension area and the Torrey Pines State Reserve had finally become a complete geological and ecological unit. Eventually, the valley behind Del Mar was also saved when the cities of San Diego and Del Mar established the Crest Canyon Preserve in order to protect the valley and the trees from proposed development. Thus, most of the surviving groves of Torrey Pines in the world had been preserved.

Figure 4–*The road through the Reserve still resembles this 1918 picture as it winds its way up past High Point to the Lodge. San Diego Historical Society - Ticor Collection.*

For the dreamers and the workers the peace and tranquility, the feeling of oneness with aeons past and the unique beauty of the Extension is their well-deserved reward and recognition.

THE TORREY PINE

The following essay on the Torrey Pine (*Pinus torreyana* Parry) is adapted from a paper presented by Guy L. Fleming before the Western Society of Naturalists and the Ecological Society of America at the AAAS (Pacific Section) meeting at Pasadena in 1931.

The centuries that have passed have left us but few living relics of that age when the rainfall was at its optimum along our Southern California coast and a great forest of mixed conifers and other plants of a moist temperate climate extended from the mountains to the seashore. The Torrey Pine is an outstanding survivor of that era. Although a member of the dominant and widely distributed Coniferae of the north-temperate region, this peculiar maritime pine, in former geological times a fairly widespread species, is now so near the verge of extinction in the two limited stations where it is found that it is today among the rarest of all pines.

For the benefit of those who may not be familiar with the Torrey Pine its distinguishing characters are as follows. The leaves are in fascicles of fives and are 8 to 12 inches long. They are very large and strong, being some of the strongest pine leaves known. The staminate flowers are very large, 2 to 2½ inches long. The yearling cones are about an inch long on peduncles 1 to 2 inches long. The second season cones become ovate, symmetrical, and 2½ to 3½ inches in length. The third year, when mature, they are broadly ovate, symmetrical, and 4 to 6 inches long. The scales are chocolate-brown, prominently pyramidal, and are capped with a small, obtuse, stiff, needle-like projection. The nuts are very large, sub-cylindrical, and nearly an inch long. The dorsal surface is spotted with black areas. The seed-wing is short, very thick at the base and encases the seed, whose shell is thick and hard, requiring considerable force to fracture it; the kernels are oily and delicious to the taste. While the cones discharge most of their seeds the third year, they are somewhat persistent and usually do not fall from the tree until the fifth or sixth year, when they break away leaving a few lower undeveloped scales on the branchlet.

Figure 5–*View to the west from Torrey Pines Extension: Los Peñasquitos Lagoon and north bluffs of the Reserve.*

The main forest extends, in scattered groups, along the coast from the San Dieguito estuary at Del Mar, southward about five miles. The best stands are located in the rugged, broken ravines and along the bluffs on either side of Los Peñasquitos estuary and on the cliff slopes above the sea. The trees grow upon a crumbling, soft sand-rock, or in a sandy loam of some depth lying upon the sand-rock. There is evidence that this sand-rock is of sand dune origin. It is probable that the Torrey Pine is the remnant of some ancient dune forest.

Like other maritime pines the Torrey Pines are low in stature, their growth retarded and distorted by the prevailing sea-wind which has an average velocity of five and a half miles per hour. Yet this wind undoubtedly insures their existence in this habitat. They are saved from extinction by cool air from the heights flowing down to meet the humid sea-breeze. On the exposed cliff slopes these pines grow dwarfed and prostrate. Some creep along, espalier-shaped for 30 or 40 feet, their bowed limbs often overlaid with soil, from which they send up short, twisted, leaf-tufted branches. Others hang suspended on the edge of canyon cliffs, their exposed, bark-covered, main roots running far down the face of the cliff to secure a foot-hold and nourishment from some soil ledge below. On the sheltered inner side of the hills, and on the spurs of the cross ravines the trees attain the greatest size, a few measuring 2½ feet in trunk diameter and carrying their flattened crowns to a height of 50 to 60 feet.

The relatively low and irregular precipitation, with an average seasonal rainfall of less than 11 inches, seriously affects the perpetuation of these pines. Years of uniform rainfall stimulate fruiting and germination, but they are too often followed by years of irregular rainfall, and by periods of drought and high temperatures. At such times the mortality among seedlings and young trees is so high that it offsets any gain made during favorable seasons. In response to these extreme changes the trees develop extensive root systems. Seedlings just out of the ground send their roots to a depth of three feet or more. In older trees, feeder roots may be found 200 feet from the main stem, penetrating to a depth of 15 feet in the sand-rock.

Upon Santa Rosa Island the Torrey Pines live under better conditions. The rainfall averages are higher than at the mainland station and the island is frequently shrouded in fog. The pine trees, therefore, are much more robust and vigorous than on the mainland. They bear larger and heavier cones, which contain large, somewhat flattened seeds. Some trees on Santa Rosa Island attain a trunk diameter of over three feet. It has been suggested that they may be a distinct subspecies.

There are many tall, tree-like shrubs, native to the Reserve, that grow among the pines and in the canyons. The most numerous are the Lemonadeberry (Figure 6) and the Laurel-leaf Sumac. Even taller than these are the Toyon or Christmas-Berry (Figure 7) and the California Scrub Oak. The Warty-Stem Ceanothus (Figure 8) grows in abundance in the Reserve. It is a

Figure 6—*LEMONADEBERRY. A medium-sized evergreen shrub with dark-green oval leaves and stout twigs. It has white to pinkish flowers arranged in close panicles. The fruit is a flat berry with an acid, viscous coating. A cooling but acrid drink can be made from the fruits. Lemonadeberry is abundant along the trails throughout the Reserve. It belongs to the Sumac family; blooms February-May.*

Figure 7–*CHRISTMAS-BERRY OR TOYON. A large, bushy, evergreen shrub. The leaves are oblong or elliptical, thick, leathery, and dark-green. The flowers are white, small and in clusters. The fruits are bright-red berries, often used at Christmas time for decorations. There are plants of Toyon at the entrance to the Guy Fleming Trail. Toyon belongs to the Rose family; blooms June-July.*

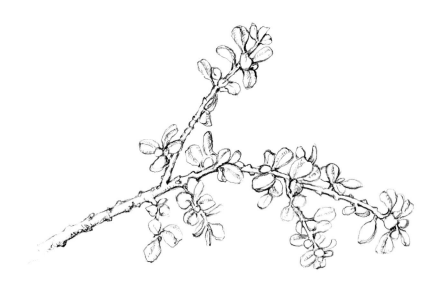

Figure 8–WARTY-STEM CEANOTHUS. *A stiff-branched, rounded, evergreen shrub. It has dark-green leaves, and white flowers arranged in dense clusters. It is quite showy in the spring. The stems are studded with wart-like excrescences. It is found near the Lodge and on the trails. Ceanothus belongs to the Buckthorn family; blooms January-April.*

lovely shrub with white flowers, and is commonly called White Lilac. It is, however, not a lilac, in spite of a superficial resemblance. The Mission Manzanita (Figure 9) is a smaller shrub with reddish manzanita bark and small, urn-shaped flowers that simulate tiny pink and white bells. Two other medium-sized shrubs are Mountain-Mahogany and the Goodding Willow.

Among the small shrubs that cover the hillsides are the widespread Chamise or Greasewood and the California Sagebrush. In spring, Greasewood is covered with masses of small white flowers. The California Sagebrush has small, inconspicuous flowers. It is fragrant and spicy but quite different botanically from the true sages. The true sages are widely distributed in the Reserve. The White Sage, the Black Sage (Figure 10), whose leaves can be used for flavoring, and the Cleveland Sage with its clear-blue flowers, are commonly seen.

One of the most elegant shrubs in the Reserve is the Tree Poppy. It has beautiful four-petaled yellow blossoms that look like large, yellow butterflies. It grows to a height of five or six feet and is known to be difficult to cultivate in the garden. A common shrub, called Bushrue or Spice Bush (Figure 11) has fine delicate leaves. In the spring it produces little, white, star-like flowers. In the summer, the small citrus-like berries are first yellow, then

Figure 9—*MISSION MANZANITA. An erect, densely branched, evergreen shrub, with grayish-brown, shredding bark and ash-colored branchlets. The dark-green leaves are oval. The flowers are white or pink, urn-shaped, and resemble tiny bells. It is found on the Guy Fleming Trail, and it belongs to the Heather family; blooms December-February.*

red, and finally black. Spotted in many places under the trees is Mojave Yucca or Spanish Dagger (Bayonet), an unusual but handsome shrub.

California Buckwheat (Figure 12) is abundant and always decorative with its myriad of white blossoms in the late spring. These flowers, as they dry in summer and fall, become a rich golden-brown. On the ocean front along the cliff edge one finds the yellow-flowered, ill-scented Bladderpod, a small shrub. In the same habitat are three kinds of cactus: the Coast Barrel Cactus which grows slightly above the surface of the ground, the Coastal Prickly-Pear, and the Coastal Cholla.

Figure 10–*BLACK SAGE. An erect shrub, openly branched and approximately 5 feet high. The leaves are green, wrinkled above, and very aromatic. They are often used for flavoring. The flowers are in compact whorls forming interrupted clusters on the stems. They are usually pale-blue to lavender. There are plants of this species at the entrance to the Guy Fleming Trail. It belongs to the Mint family; blooms April-June.*

Other conspicuous plants are the Red Monkey-Flower (Figure 13), Deerweed, and Golden Yarrow. Among the small, low-growing plants are the Canchalagua, Mariposa Lily, the Ground Pink, Lupine, Blue-eyed Grass, Shooting Star, and Milk-maids. (See Appendix for more complete list.)

The wildflower display in the spring varies with the amount of winter rain, but usually one or more species will appear in great abundance, particularly on the cliffs above the surf. One year it may be a spectacular display of the golden California Poppy accompanied by the Evening Primrose, the white flowers of the Rosin Weed (or Three-Spot), and Tidy Tips, whose ray florets are light yellow outlined in white. In other years the abundant pink flowers of the Seaside Sand-Verbena may be dominant. The most striking of all the perennial flowers in the Reserve is the Sea-Dahlia (Figure 14). It grows luxuriantly under the trees and produces a brilliant display of large yellow flowers each spring.

Figure 11–*SPICE BUSH. A strong-scented, much branched shrub, 2 or 3 feet high. The linear leaves are crowded at the ends of short lateral branchlets. They are yellowish-green ½ to 1 inch long. The flowers are white, small, and four-petaled. The berries are round, yellow-green to red, with citrus-like skin. It grows under the pines and along the trails. Spice Bush belongs to the Rue family; blooms November-March.*

Figure 12–*CALIFORNIA BUCKWHEAT. A low spreading shrub, with long, leafy branches. The leaves are in dense bundles or fascicles; green above, white-wooly beneath, and linear. The flowers are arranged in white or pinkish clusters at the end of the stems. This species is confined to the coastal region and is very much at home under the Torrey Pines. It occurs throughout the Reserve. It belongs to the Buckwheat family; blooms May-October.*

Figure 13–*RED MONKEY-FLOWER. A freely branched, erect shrub, 3 to 5 feet high. The leaves are dark-green and sticky above, linear, elliptic, and finely toothed. The flowers are long, tubular, orange-red to brick-red. A closely related species, <u>Mimulus flemingii</u> Munz, grows under the Torrey Pines on Santa Rosa Island. The Monkey-Flower belongs to the Figwort family; blooms March-July.*

Figure 14—*SEA-DAHLIA. A robust, erect perennial with a fern-like appearance; 2 to 3 feet high, growing from a tuberous tap root. The leaves are green, linear, and widely divided. The flowers are on long stems, and are rich-yellow, similar to garden coreopsis. The plants grow profusely and widely under the pine trees, where they thrive. This species belongs to the Composite or Sunflower family; blooms March-May.*

In addition to the flowering plants, there are several species of ferns, growing on the shady sides of the canyons facing the sea. Among them are: California Maidenhair Fern, Coast Wood Fern, Coffee Fern, Goldenback Fern, and California Polypody.

Those interested can obtain more information on the plants at the Reserve Headquarters.

ASSOCIATED ANIMALS

INSECTS

Insects are not common in the Torrey Pines area. The cool climate and ocean winds preclude flight of the preponderant small forms, and many groups are nocturnal. Fortunately the "nuisance varieties" such as flies, fleas, and mosquitos are scarce.

Because of their bright colors and diurnal habits butterflies are the insects most likely to be seen in the Reserve. The largest and most conspicuous is the Western Tiger Swallowtail with its bright yellow, black-barred wings. Willow and poplar are the chief food plants of its caterpillars. The Anise Swallowtail is a darkly colored form with the yellow and black bars and spots on its wings evenly distributed. It is frequently seen flying in open areas skirting the pines. Its handsome green, black, and yellow caterpillars feed on Sweet Fennel, an introduced European weed of the Carrot family.

The white Cabbage Butterfly is occasionally seen. This immigrant from Europe prefers cultivated areas where it lays eggs on cabbage, kale, and brussels sprouts.

Orange-tips are a large group of early spring fliers. They are showy butterflies distinguished by bright orange-tipped forewings. The Sara Orange-tip is the only one likely to be seen in the Reserve. The caterpillars feed on wild mustard, but prefer the smaller and rarer forms of the Mustard family.

During the spring and summer the yellow, black-bordered Sulphur Butterflies scurry through the Reserve. Boisduval's Sulphur is the most common. Its larvae are pests on alfalfa and clover. Occasionally in the late summer and fall the bright, orange-yellow Nicippe Yellow may be seen as it searches for Cassia, a yellow-flowered plant of the Pea family.

Figure 15–*Pine trees, cacti and chaparral in an open area of the Reserve. The spiny Spanish Dagger produces tall spikes of white flowers in the spring.*

41

The larvae of the Monarch Butterfly feed only on milkweeds. It overwinters in this area after long migration from northern states. The Monarch's bright red-brown wings, with black veins, and its leisurely flight, make it a conspicuous insect. Birds have learned not to touch the Monarch because it has an offensive acrid taste.

Another spangled beauty is the Gulf Fritillary. It is distinguished by bright silver spots on the underside of the wings. Its larval food plant is Passion Vine (*Passiflora* sp.) which is not native. When the plant was introduced from the Gulf States and Mexico, the butterfly followed. Since Passion Vine is not found in the Reserve, this butterfly is a passerby only.

The Mourning Cloak is a large, handsome, black-velvety butterfly with yellow-bordered wings. It is frequently seen resting on a perch from whence it can dart out and chase a passing insect. The black spiny caterpillars of Mourning Cloak feed on willow, elm, poplar, and other trees.

One California Sister, a rare Nymphalid butterfly, was found in a spider web. Its larvae feed exclusively on oak. Checker-spots, Blues, Metal-marks, and Skippers are occasionally seen, but they are smaller and less conspicuous than most other butterflies.

There are more species of moths in the Reserve than there are butterflies, but they are mostly nocturnal. Countless small insects, other than Lepidoptera, could be found by the serious student with time to seek them out.

One large Scarabaeid Beetle, commonly called the Rain Beetle, is of special interest to scientists because of its rarity and unusual habits. The male is large and jet black. The female is one-third again larger than the male and is brown. Unlike the male, it cannot fly. The beetles spend all but a few minutes of their life-span of two or more years underground, where as larvae, they feed on rootlets. Mating occurs only after a soaking rain has softened the ground. Then, for a few minutes only, in the rain, usually in the early morning or late evening, the male takes flight. A female waits at the entrance of her burrow until a flying male has caught her scent and comes to earth: they then mate underground.

Various pests attack the Torrey Pine trees: mites, scale insects and beetles may be involved. Normally, if the trees are healthy and vigorous they are able to withstand such attacks.

During the late 1980's drought conditions in Southern California caused steady deterioration of the environment in the Reserve and the presence of the Five-spined Engraver Beetle (*Ips paraconfusus*) has become a major factor in the

Figure 16—*Elegantly eroded sandstone ridge with a straight, young Torrey Pine and an older, flat-crowned tree.*

loss of trees, especially in the western groves. This bark beetle occurs throughout California and southern Oregon and causes damage to pine trees of many species. It is a small beetle (4-5mm) which bores through the bark, makes egg chambers in the cambium layer and lays its eggs. The hatching larvae chew more cambium, pupate and emerge as adults to continue the cycle. If the cambium layer is stripped, the tree dies. Healthy trees, with adequate sap pressure, can cope with the attacking adult beetle but trees under stress from drought, soil compaction, fire damage, etc. are not able to do so.

Considering other environmental factors to which the trees are subjected in an urban area, the most reasonable approach to dealing with this problem (as of 1991) seems to be one which involves trapping the adult beetles rather than removal of infested trees or other impractical remedies such as watering or poisoning.

Not all of the insects are destructive. The Lady-bug Beetle, found in the Reserve, is beneficial because it feeds on scale insects and mites.

AMPHIBIANS AND REPTILES

The Torrey Pines State Reserve, since it lacks freshwater streams and ponds, is not an optimum habitat for amphibians. They are usually inconspicuous and are not well documented. The list of frogs, toads and salamanders which may be encountered is in the Appendix.

Reptiles are more likely to find the Reserve a favorable habitat and the small lizards are frequently seen resting in the sun or scurrying into the underbrush. The commonest lizard is the small California Side-blotched Lizard named for the black spot on its side though the females lack this feature. Additionally, one often sees the Western Fence Lizard which is about 3 inches long and dusky-brown or gray above with dark blotches. There may be a blue patch on the throat and belly sides. Skinks are often heard amongst the dry leaves and resemble tiny snakes with their smooth, slim bodies.

Snakes are sometimes seen especially on the paths through the Reserve, the commonest being the San Diego Gopher Snake and the California Kingsnake. The former is a large yellow or cream-colored snake with black, brown or reddish blotches and a dark line across the head. The latter is smaller and has alternating rings of plain black or dark brown and white or pale yellow. In wetter areas the Two-striped Garter Snake can be found. It is small, plain olive or grayish-brown above, with dark spots underneath and lateral stripes.

Two species of rattlesnakes are found in the Reserve: the Southern Pacific, which is light-colored with brown or black blotches, and the Red Diamond, which is diamond-patterned in a red coloration. Both can be clearly recognized by the triangular-shaped head and the tail rattles. They are not usually aggressive but are dangerous when suddenly disturbed. The sound of the rattle should be a warning to stay clear! They are most common in the spring and summer months since they hibernate during the winter.

Marine turtles may wander along the Southern California coast but are rarely seen.

BIRDS

The bird watcher will find a visit to Torrey Pines State Reserve a rewarding experience. There are birds that haunt the chaparral, forage among the trees and in the canyons, nest in the cliffs, and feed along the beaches. There are also shorebirds and waterfowl which reside in the estuary or stop there for food and rest during their migratory flight. Many of the species of birds recorded for the Reserve are listed on the Checklist which is available at the Reserve Headquarters. Waterfowl and shorebirds may be found in greatly increased numbers at the estuary during migration, especially in the fall. The peak month is usually October, and when the weather and the condition of the estuary suits their needs, a sizable number reside for the winter.

Approximately 65 species may be found in the Reserve any time of the year, with nesting species being augmented by lingering migrants or post-nesting visitors. The species most apt to be seen by the visiting birder at any season include the following:

Pied-billed Grebe	White-throated Swift
Double-crested Cormorant	Anna's Hummingbird
Great Blue Heron	Black Phoebe
Great Egret	Scrub Jay
Snowy Egret	Common Raven
Black-crowned Night Heron	Bushtit
Mallard	Wrentit
Gadwall	California Thrasher
Red-tailed Hawk	Loggerhead Shrike
American Coot	Starling
Snowy Plover	Common Yellowthroat
Killdeer	Rufous-sided Towhee
Willet	California Towhee
Marbled Godwit	Savannah Sparrow
Ring-billed Gull	Song Sparrow
Western Gull	Red-winged Blackbird
Forster's Tern	Brewer's Blackbird
Rock Dove	House Finch
Mourning Dove	Lesser Goldfinch

Some of the most brilliantly colored western birds migrate through the Reserve. Examples of these include the Rufous Hummingbird, Western Kingbird, Western Bluebird, Black-throated Gray Warbler, Northern Oriole, Western Tanager, Black-headed Grosbeak, Lazuli Bunting, and Lawrence's Goldfinch. There are other flycatchers, warblers and vireos as indicated in the Checklist.

The stiff, leathery-leaved chaparral is ideal for sheltering the Wrentit, California Towhee, Rufous-sided Towhee, California Thrasher, and the Rufous-crowned Sparrow. In fall, winter, and spring it also shelters the White-crowned Sparrow, Golden-crowned Sparrow and an occasional Fox Sparrow.

Along the edges of the estuary one will find Savannah Sparrows, Song Sparrows, Blackbirds, Marsh Wrens, Yellowthroats, and in the proper season, Lincoln's Sparrows, various flycatchers and other passerine species.

The less frequented stretches of beach at the base of the 350-foot cliffs offer a magnificent view of shorebirds. It is fascinating to watch the active little Sanderlings keep one step ahead of the waves (Figure 17). They seem to flow back and forth with the rhythm of the surf. One can also watch Western Gulls, Ring-billed Gulls and Brown Pelicans plane overhead on the cliffside thermals. A winter visitor to the area will also find Glaucous-winged Gulls, Herring Gulls, California Gulls, Mew Gulls, Bonaparte's Gulls, and Heermann's Gulls which come up from Mexico. Numerous shorebirds may be found along the beaches or on the mudflats along the estuary. From the cliffs one may occasionally see pelagic species such as shearwaters, petrels and jaegers.

Some of the more spectacular birds that can be found in the estuary and marsh include terns, egrets, herons, Long-billed Curlews, American Avocets, Black-necked Stilts, and at the proper time of year, numerous waterfowl. The importance of keeping the estuary and surrounding marsh open to the sea and in its natural condition cannot be over-emphasized. Man-made "improvements" cause an ever-increasing need for the protection of those birds which depend upon marsh areas for their survival. (See section on **Birds of the Lagoon.**)

LAND MAMMALS

Since many land mammals are nocturnal, they will not often be seen by the visitor to the Reserve. The Beechey Ground Squirrel is probably the most commonly observed mammal in the Reserve because it is active during the daylight hours. Ground squirrels are fairly common along the beach but less so

Figure 17–*Sanderlings feeding on the beach at the water edge (from a color lithograph by George M. Mattson).*

47

in the upland areas. They prefer dry, rocky soil for burrowing. Rapid reproduction rates can turn these pretty animals into pests.

The Black-tailed Jackrabbit, the Brush Rabbit and the Audubon Cottontail are commonly seen. The Jackrabbit, really a hare, is the largest of these three related species. The long ears and black tail will identify it immediately. The Brush Rabbit is the darker of the smaller rabbits and is not found far from cover. The Audubon Cottontail may be in sparse cover or even in the open.

Gray Foxes may be seen running across the roads or trails during the day though most of their activity is at night. Small tracks with clear claw marks are an indication that they are present and probably quite common. They feed mostly on rodents but are not averse to scavenging table scraps or raiding garbage cans. Manzanita and Toyon berries are also very acceptable in season.

Two other small mammals, the Spotted Skunk and the Striped Skunk, are sometimes active during the day. They also raid garbage cans and occasionally trap themselves inside. Skunks use their well-known spray only as a last defense or when taken by surprise.

The Long-tailed Weasel is most likely to be seen in the area near the lagoon and it is active during the day. This weasel is about the size of a large rat and has a long, yellow-brown body. It is an active, agile and skilled hunter feeding mostly on rodents which are killed by biting through the skull. It has a strong, distinctive odor. A Virginia Opossum may be seen hanging from a tree limb by its long prehensile tail. Opossums are omnivorous and co-exist happily with humans.

The most abundant mammals are those least often seen. Tell-tale mounds indicate the presence of subterranean Pocket Gophers and Moles. Pocket Mice and three or four species of White-footed Mice come out at night. In the thicker brush Woodrats construct houses and venture forth only after dark. In the grassy and marshy lower area of the Reserve one might see Meadow Mice, Harvest Mice and, occasionally, Shrews. Several kinds of bats come out after night-flying insects.

Coyote and Bobcat which live nearby come into the park in search of rabbits and rodents. A few Mule Deer may be seen feeding near the Lagoon in the late afternoon or early morning.

Figure 18–*Cliff promontory with the end of the Beach Trail cutting diagonally across it near Flat Rock. Fossil oyster beds can be seen here in rocks of the Del Mar Formation.*

LOS PEÑASQUITOS MARSH
NATURAL PRESERVE AND LAGOON

THE PHYSICAL ENVIRONMENT

The lagoon-marsh complex constitutes the northern part of the Reserve. The marsh is now carefully protected under its designation as a Natural Preserve. The area was formed about 10 to 20 thousand years ago as a result of the melting of the polar ice caps at the end of the Fourth Glacial Period. As the sea rose, it flooded the valley cut by the young Los Peñasquitos River to form a deep embayment. Since that time, however, the sediment brought down by the river has filled in most of the valley, forming extensive mudflats so that now only relatively shallow channels and broad tidal pans remain (Figures 5, 19 and 20). During earlier periods, considerably more fresh water must have entered the lagoon than at the present time, because while describing Portola's trek from San Diego to Monterey in July 1769, Fr. Crespi spoke of the Soledad Valley (Sorrento Valley) as being "very green and grassy." He also described a small village of Indians "with little straw houses" and a pool of water in an arroyo near the village.

Fresh water now enters the lagoon from several sources. Although most of the natural drainage flows through Los Peñasquitos Canyon, during periods of high rainfall some water enters the basin from Carmel Valley to the north and from Sorrento Valley to the south. The total watershed draining into Los Peñasquitos Lagoon is approximately 60,000 acres. In addition, water in the form of treated sewage effluent has been entering the southeast portion from two nearby sewage treatment plants. In 1970 plans were formalized for the discharge of the wastes through the Metropolitan Sewage System.

Evidence from the configuration of the major lagoon channels indicates the original ocean entrance to have been at the extreme southwest corner of the lagoon, where the south parking lot stands today. Later, however, the opening tended to meander northward so that when the first narrow-gauge railroad was constructed in 1888 along the north side of the valley, railroad maps show the ocean entrance to be at the extreme northwest edge of the valley under the present northernmost highway bridge. The old McGonigle Road constructed in 1909 wound its way northward down the Torrey Pines Grade and along the sand dunes, crossing the lagoon near the present entrance.

Figure 19—*Los Peñasquitos Marsh Natural Preserve and Lagoon. View looking north across lagoon from the road winding up to the lodge.*

INTERSTATE 5

SORRENTO VALLEY ROAD

SALT PAN

SALT PAN

SALT PAN

SALT FLAT

CREEK

OXIDATION POND

N E W S

CARMEL VALLEY ROAD

SALT PAN

6' CONTOUR

MUD FLAT

LA JOLLA

OLD HIGHWAY 101 S 21

MUD FLAT

PARKING LOT

PARKING

TO THE TORREY PINES LODGE

BEACH

RELIC SAND DUNE

PACIFIC OCEAN

52

Until 1925, man had not greatly interfered with the normal lagoon drainage. Then however, the building of the present Santa Fe Railroad caused the first damage. The new roadbed running through the center of the valley divided the lagoon into its present northeast and southwest portions, significantly altering the tidal-current pattern. This alteration decreased the effective tidal flow to approximately one quarter of its pre-1925 values, so that by 1928, photographs showed the entrance channel to be choked with sand as far as the old McGonigle Road Bridge. When the coast highway was expanded in the 1930's, the low beach barrier was increased in height for the roadbed and the lagoon entrance was shifted southward one quarter mile to its present location near the old McGonigle Bridge. Most of the old bridge pilings have been removed to increase tidal flow but at low tide some of them may still be seen.

Apparently during earlier periods the combination of higher rainfall together with a larger lagoon area and a less restricted entrance provided sufficient flow to keep a channel open through to the beach. Such a continuous connection with the sea is important for the survival of a normal lagoon flora and fauna. Evidence supplied by the abundant remains of shellfish and other marine life found in nearby Indian kitchen middens indicates that the lagoon mouth was permanently open thousands of years ago. Under present conditions, however, a permanent opening cannot be naturally maintained and the marine life has diminished and at times has been almost eliminated. During exceptionally wet winters sufficient runoff may accumulate in the lagoon to break through the barrier bar naturally. If the bar is not breached in this manner the channel is often bulldozed open to alleviate the danger of flooding and to improve the health of the lagoon.

The recent history of Los Peñasquitos and most other Southern California lagoons has been one of short periods of connection with the sea, alternating with longer periods of stagnation. With the stopping of the normal tidal ebb and flow, evaporation during periods of negligible freshwater inflow may increase salinities to high values. One such period occurred in January, 1959, when a combination of high tides and storm waves carried sand high enough up the berm to block the channel. As a result, the salinity steadily increased over an eight-month interval from a normal value of 34 parts per thousand (‰) to 63‰. The salt content was so high that only a few hardy species of marine animals were able to survive. These were the California Killifish, the Bay Topsmelt and the California Mudsucker. Most of the other abundant fish and shellfish fauna that had flourished when the lagoon was open to the sea disappeared.

Figure 20–*Los Peñasquitos Marsh Natural Preserve*

On the other hand, if the amount of fresh water added should exceed the amount lost by evaporation, the seawater may be excessively diluted causing distress to truly marine forms. The addition of sewage effluent (which began in 1962) lowered the surface salinity to approximately 13‰ by late 1966. Although low salt content in the surface water inhibited many species, the deeper waters retained a salinity approximately that of seawater, furnishing a tolerable habitat for a few marine forms. Although not optimal for strictly freshwater or marine organisms, this surface brackish water is ideal for the establishment of species such as Ruppia. In 1966 this plant covered the entire lagoon surface. However, when the high rainfall in early 1967 breached the bar, the inflow of tidal seawater restored salinities to near ocean values and it gradually disappeared. This introduction of fresh seawater with its many swimming and floating organisms quickly reestablished many elements of a normal estuarine biota.

Many species of plants and animals that characterize lagoon habitats and are found in nearby lagoons have not yet established themselves in Los Peñasquitos Lagoon. Noteworthy examples among the plants are the Cord Grass (*Spartina foliosa*) and the Eelgrass (*Zostera marina*), which normally dominate the mid-marsh and subtidal zones respectively of Mission and South San Diego bays. Among the animals, the California Hornshell (*Cerithidea californica*) and the Smooth Chione (*Chione fluctifraga*), which are abundant in these same marsh zones in Mission and South San Diego bays, are conspicuously absent in Los Peñasquitos marsh.

Some of these plants and animals are known to have been present in Los Peñasquitos Lagoon in former times. For example, Chione is one of the most abundant shellfish in the nearby Indian kitchen middens and Cord Grass was recorded from the lagoon during a vegetation survey made in 1942.

Dissolved oxygen, needed for most biological activity, is generally high during the day in the surface waters but becomes very low at night. This reflects considerable photosynthesis during the daylight hours and excessive respiration and decomposition (which use up oxygen) in the dark. The low values found in bottom waters indicate high rates of organic decomposition and correspondingly high productivity rates. The plant nutrients (nitrate and phosphate) are high in the lagoon compared with coastal water, presumably because of the continuous input of sewage effluent. These nutrients stimulate copious plant growth, particularly when the lagoon is closed from the sea.

The lagoon environment is thus a highly variable habitat compared with the open ocean. It is not surprising that to survive in such an unstable environment, plants and animals must have considerably more tolerance than either their marine or freshwater relatives. In addition, many species have

54

evolved specialized structures and behavior patterns to survive these extreme conditions.

SALT MARSH PLANTS

At first glance, the plant life of the Torrey Pines Lagoon appears to be unexciting. The salt marsh plants are almost all low-growing and lacking in brightly colored flowers. These drab-looking plants, however, merit far greater attention than they normally receive because they exhibit some beautiful examples of ecological adaptation. Existing midway between the marine environment of seaweeds and the land environment of the upland scrub, the salt marsh plants have evolved the ability to cope with both salt water submergence and long hours of exposure to sun and wind.

The key to the success of salt marsh plants is their ability to thrive in highly saline soil. Unlike their upland ancestors, which cannot survive if the salinity of the soil water rises above 5‰, the salt marsh plants may grow in soil salinities of up to 80‰. Some species, such as Salt Grass and Glasswort, can survive even in environments where the soil surface is covered with a crust of salt crystals.

These salt marsh plants have adopted several different devices to enable them to overcome adverse salinity. Many species dilute the salt in their cells by storing large amounts of water; as a consequence, the plants are fleshy and resemble desert succulents rather than plants of an aquatic environment. Other salt marsh species rid themselves of salt by pumping it out through tiny glands that cover their leaves. A few of these plants store salt in their lower leaves, which are subsequently shed.

Another important adaptation of salt marsh plants is their ability to tolerate the water-logged, clayey marsh soils that are frequently deficient in oxygen. Many of the salt marsh plants store air in large spaces in their roots and underground stems; some appear to have an internal ventilation system through which oxygen travels from the leaves to the smallest rootlets. The spreading underground network of salt marsh plant roots plays an important role in binding the muddy sediments of the marshland, thus preventing rapid erosion.

Approximately 30 species of salt marsh plants occur in Los Peñasquitos Lagoon. These species tend to be grouped into contoured zones or belts of vegetation that correspond with average tidal levels in the marsh (Figure 21). At the lowest tidal level in Los Peñasquitos salt marsh (closest to the lagoon channels), an abundance of Pickleweed (Figure 22) and patches of Alkali Heath are found. The Pickleweed (and related *Salicornia* species) has succulent, jointed stems and tiny leaves that are reduced to membrane-fringed triangles

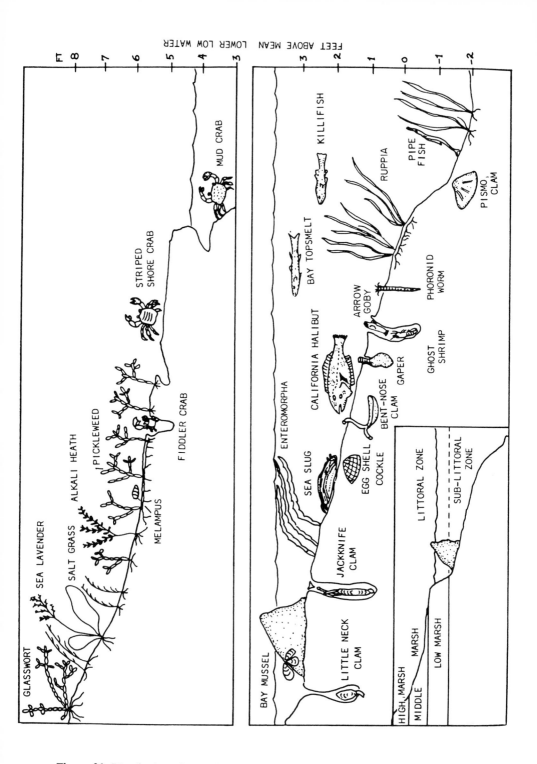

Figure 21–*Distribution of animals and plants in Los Peñasquitos Lagoon according to tidal height.*

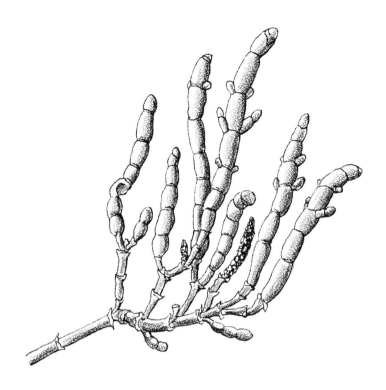

Figure 22–*Pickleweed, a characteristic plant of the lagoon.*

clasping the stem nodes. The flowers are minute and remain more or less embedded in the fleshy stems; only the yellow pollen sacs and the delicate white pollen-receiving stigmas emerge from the stem, turning the flower-bearing shoots into yellow or white fairy dusters in late summer. The Alkali Heath can be recognized by its dark-green leaves, the edges of which are down-rolled. In late spring and summer, this plant becomes clothed in delicate rose-pink flowers which are avidly sought by bees.

At higher elevations in the marsh (that area covered by salt water only during the high spring tides), several other plants appear among the Pickleweed and Alkali Heath. These high-marsh plants include Salt Grass, Sea Lavender and California Seablite. The Salt Grass is characterized by slender, sickle-shaped leaves that roll tightly inward during dry conditions. The Sea Lavender is most easily recognized in mid-summer when it sends up long shoots bearing filmy sprays of pale-violet flowers in the center of a cluster of broad, leathery leaves. These leaves (and those of the Salt Grass and Alkali Heath) are frequently coated with a white film of salt that has been pumped out of the plant by an efficient method of biological desalination. In contrast to the Salt Grass and Sea Lavender, the short, densely packed leaves of the California Seablite are devoid of salt glands but are swollen with water that is used to dilute the internally stored salt. The greenish flowers of the Seablite are small and inconspicuous; however, the leaves of this plant turn orange-pink in late summer, forming a feathery splash of soft color.

The uppermost zone of the marsh is wetted only by extreme high spring tides and by storm waves. This zone is generally marked by the presence of Glasswort. This plant is a succulent-stemmed shrub, similar in appearance to Pickleweed but brighter green, and with shorter, more slender stem segments. On the southeast side of Los Peñasquitos Lagoon, where the upper lagoon channels give way to broad areas of bare salt pans, the Glasswort is often accompanied by two attractive spring annuals. One of these annuals, the Salt Marsh Daisy, forms conspicuous carpets of golden blossoms in early spring, following a good winter rain. Later in spring, Little Ice-plant appears with sprays of tiny white flowers and leaves dotted by crystal-like water-storing glands; as summer approaches, the flowers disappear but the color of the leaves ripens into an attractive orange-red hue.

On the southwest side of the Torrey Pines marshland, where the fresh water of Los Peñasquitos Creek mingles with the saline lagoon water, the salt marsh vegetation gives way to a group of plants that are adapted to brackish-water conditions. Most conspicuous of these plants are Cat-tails, large clumps of Spiny Rush that resemble over-grown porcupines, and low-growing mats of Brass-Buttons, which, as their name suggests, are dotted with small, golden, disc-like flowers during much of the year.

The upland edge of the Torrey Pines salt marsh, above the direct influence of tidal water, grades into typical coastal scrub vegetation. In this "transition zone" one will usually encounter familiar shrubs such as Lemonadeberry, Goldenbush, and Deerweed; these plants are also common in the main area of the Reserve.

On the southwestern side of the lagoon, near the highway, the upland border takes the form of an old sand dune that probably formed the inland portion of the Torrey Pines beach prior to the construction of the highway (Figure 20). This stabilized sand-dune area is of interest because it represents a relict of the once-extensive system of dunes that formerly lined the Southern California beaches. (Other relicts occur at the mouths of the Tijuana, San Dieguito, and San Marcos rivers and in Camp Pendleton.) At Los Peñasquitos, the most conspicuous among the plants are the sand-dune Evening Primrose, the Coastal Cholla, and the Coastal Prickly-Pear. These plants also occur on the bluffs in the main Reserve area. Two species of plants grow on the sand dune that cannot be found elsewhere in the Reserve and are also very rare in Southern California: the Beach Lotus, which is a spring annual with a spreading, mat-like growth form bearing small 3 to 5-fingered leaves and clusters of tiny orange and red pea-shaped flowers and the Golden Aster, a low-growing perennial, which can be recognized by its silver-haired leaves and daisy-like, yellow flowers that appear in early fall.

INVERTEBRATES OF THE LAGOON

Of the invertebrates occurring in the lagoon (see Appendix), the more common and interesting ones are illustrated in Figure 23. The Bay Mussel, which attains a length of 4 inches, is wedge-shaped and blue-black. It is found attached by long fibrous threads to the pilings of the railroad bridge and to the rip-rap near the northern beach parking lot. This is the "edible" mussel, prized by seafood connoisseurs. However, potential consumers of the Bay Mussel and the related open-coast California Mussel are warned not to eat them during the summer months. At this time Public Health authorities proclaim that their flesh may be poisonous because the food of the mussel may include noxious microscopic "red-tide" planktonic organisms which occasionally flourish during the warmer months.

The Common Littleneck Clam has many well-developed radiating ribs and a few, less prominent, concentric ridges. The exterior is white to yellow or tan with or without V-shaped brown markings. This clam may reach a size of 3 inches and typically is found buried in black muddy sand.

The Jackknife Clam resembles a long and narrow whitish-gray pocket knife, in life partially covered by tough brown skin. This covering protects the shell from dissolution from acid conditions in the sediments. It is rare to common and is used as fish bait locally. This clam was much more abundant during earlier periods as indicated by the many empty shells in the sediments.

The Striped Shore Crab is dark green with numerous wavy stripes along its back. This is the largest of the common lagoon crabs, reaching 3 inches in width, and often may ben seen scurrying about out of water, scavenging for food.

The Mud-flat Crab is smaller than the Shore Crab, and can be readily distinguished from it by the yellowish buff color, and by the presence of many hairs on the walking legs.

The Fiddler Crab is slightly smaller than the Mud-flat Crab and is easily recognized from the others by its stalked eyes and by the one large claw brandished by the males. During courtship this claw is waved back and forth, thus suggesting the crab's name.

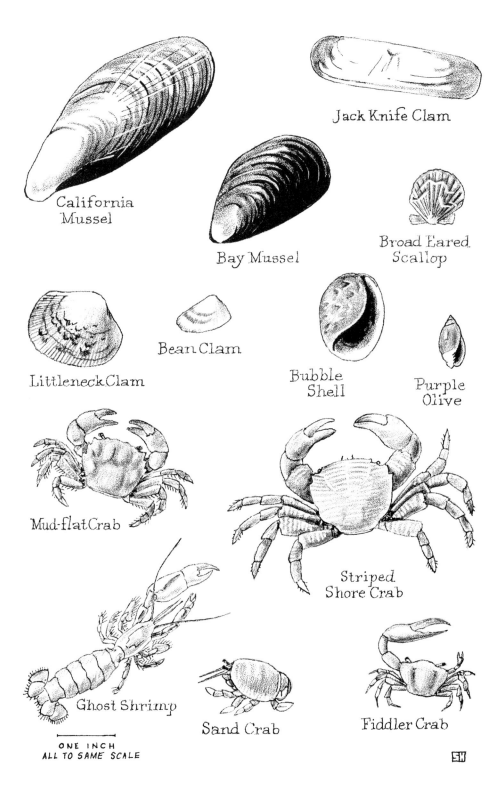

Jack Knife Clam

California
Mussel

Bay Mussel

Broad Eared
Scallop

Littleneck Clam

Bean Clam

Bubble
Shell

Purple
Olive

Mud-flat Crab

Striped
Shore Crab

Ghost Shrimp

ONE INCH
ALL TO SAME SCALE

Sand Crab

Fiddler Crab

FISHES OF THE LAGOON

At least 15 kinds of fish have been found in the shallow pools and channels of the lagoon (see Appendix). The more common species are described below.

The California Killifish is a small olive-green fish with a flattened head. It grows to 5 inches in length and may be very abundant, particularly in shallow waters. It is highly salt-tolerant, resisting the high salt concentrations when the lagoon is closed off from the sea.

The California Halibut is a flatfish, having eyes either on the left or right side of the head. The upper surface of this fish is greenish brown, sometimes mottled with small white spots. This is a commercially important food and sport fish, which, in offshore waters, may reach 5 feet in length and weigh 60 pounds. Breeding occurs in coastal waters and the juveniles make their way into bays and lagoons such as Los Peñasquitos, which they use as nursery grounds.

The Bay Topsmelt has a silvery lateral stripe and a transparent-greenish dorsal surface. This common and hardy fish lives in schools and may grow to a length of 8 inches.

The Mudsucker has a long, slender, slimy dull-olive body with a yellowish belly. It grows to 8 inches in length, and is common but usually difficult to find since it hides in the channel banks and hibernates in the bottom mud during the winter months. This extremely hardy fish will live for a week or more out of water if kept in damp seaweed. This characteristic makes the species valuable as live bait.

The Pipefishes, like the related seahorses, are biological curiosities in that the males have a brood pouch in which the females deposit eggs and the young undergo development. They occasionally reach 8 inches in length but are rare except in Ruppia beds, where, because of their coloring and shape, they may be indistinguishable from the blades of the plant.

The Southern Staghorn Sculpin has a large head with wide-set eyes and an antler-like spine in front of the gill openings. This common form may grow to a length of 6 inches. When disturbed, the spine is thrown upward and outward making a formidable defensive weapon.

The Arrow Goby is slender and small (less than 2 inches in length) and is very abundant, but because it is a sand-mud color, it is almost impossible to distinguish unless it is moving. This fish has the interesting habit of sharing the burrows of worms and ghost shrimps.

Figure 23—*Common invertebrate animals of the lagoon.*

BIRDS OF THE LAGOON

The majority of water birds which have been recorded from Los Peñasquitos Estuary are migratory waterfowl and shorebirds that rest and feed in the lagoon during their flight in fall and on their return in spring to their northern breeding grounds (see also previous section on **Birds**). The shorebirds and waders frequently may be observed probing the mudflats for worms, clams and insects at low tide or resting in the salt-pan areas at high tide. Diving birds, such as cormorants, grebes and pelicans, are most commonly seen in the deeper tidal channels near the lagoon entrance. The majority of ducks usually congregate in the large ponds on the southwest side of the lagoon where the freshwater stream enters.

Relatively few birds are permanent residents of the lagoon area. However, several showy species such as the stately Great Blue Heron, and the vociferous Black-necked Stilt and Killdeer are often seen. The Stilts and Killdeer nest on the dry salt pan area on the southwest side of the lagoon.

Several other birds are frequently seen in the lagoon area although they are not dependent on the marshland for their survival. The commonest bird in the Pickleweed vegetation is the dainty, speckle-breasted Savannah Sparrow. The flute-like tones of the Western Meadowlark, and the guttural "kwaak" of the Black-crowned Night Heron are frequently heard at the western end of the marsh and the scarlet flash of the Red-winged Blackbird is a common sight among the cat-tails and wild mustard at the eastern end of the lagoon. Two fairly common predatory birds are the slender, graceful Northern Harrier and the handsome Black-shouldered Kite; both may be seen gliding over the salt marsh in search of small rodents and birds. The Kites, which only a few years ago were in danger of extinction, are becoming commoner in the Reserve, and Red-tail and Red-shouldered Hawks, Pelicans and Ospreys are also occasional visitors.

MAMMALS OF THE LAGOON

Relatively little is known about the mammals that frequent the lagoon area since most of them are nocturnal and secretive in their movements. It is also doubtful whether any of the observed mammals are entirely dependent on the salt marsh for their existence. Most of them appear to live in the grassland, brush, and dry bank areas adjacent to the marshland and to venture forth into the marsh to forage during periods of low tides.

Most conspicuous of these mammals are the Mule Deer that graze in the salt flats south of the lagoon. Rarely seen, but evident from tracks in this salt-pan area, are the Coyote, Bobcat and Raccoon. Abundant shells in the Raccoon scats indicate that they catch and eat the crayfish that abound in the salt flat area following winter rains.

A number of small mammals appear to forage for seeds, shoots, and insects in the grassy areas of the high marsh and in the adjacent Pickleweed. These include the Ornate Shrew, a minute velvet-coated creature with a voracious appetite and a vicious temper, the dainty Western Harvest Mouse, and the dapper, white-bellied Deer Mouse. The California Meadow Mouse, Pocket Mouse and House Mouse may also occur in this area in large numbers.

Other common visitors in the upland areas of the marsh are the Audubon Cottontail and the Brush Rabbit. Ground Squirrel burrows and Pocket Gopher mounds along the railroad embankment suggest that these mammals may also forage in the marsh. (See also section on **Land Mammals**.)

CONSERVATION OF THE LAGOON AND MARSH

The flora and fauna of Los Peñasquitos Lagoon and salt marsh obviously form a very different ecological unit from that of the upland portions of the Torrey Pines State Reserve. At present this flora and fauna is not as rare as that associated with the unique Torrey Pine trees; however, the fact that the coastal lagoons and marshlands of California are rapidly dwindling under the impact of urbanization has prompted the State Division of Parks and Recreation to raise the status of Los Peñasquitos Lagoon from "State Park" (with free public access and recreational use) to that of "State Reserve" (with restricted access and usage) and now to "State Preserve" (the most restricted usage). This label, which is pinned to only the rarest and most fragile of the state-owned lands, reflects the increasing concern of ecologists and wildlife managers for the progressive destruction of coastal wetlands, a habitat vital for the preservation of migratory waterfowl and certain species of fish and shellfish.

The "Preserve" status of Los Peñasquitos Marsh and Lagoon will ensure the future protection of the lagoon flora and fauna from direct public misuse. Unfortunately, however, the natural boundaries of the lagoon ecosystem do not coincide with the fencelines of the State Preserve, but extend upstream to the watersheds of the creeks draining into the lagoon and the tops of the mesas surrounding the marshland. Here, far outside the Preserve boundaries, the removal of brush may result in erosion and the subsequent deposition of huge loads of silt in the lagoon channels; similarly, a city many miles inland may discharge sewage effluent into a creek that flows into the lagoon and thereby cause an accumulation of unnaturally high concentrations of plant nutrients in the lagoon waters.

The lagoon is thus vulnerable to far-reaching man-made changes in addition to local environmental alterations. Furthermore, the lagoon-saltmarsh complex is an extremely fragile ecosystem, the life of which depends upon the maintenance of a regular ebb and flow of tidal water. Excessive silting of the channels will hasten the closure of the lagoon mouth and will accelerate the filling-in of the marshland. Over-enrichment of the lagoon waters will spark-off unsightly algal blooms that lead to a syndrome of plant decay, oxygen depletion, fish kills, and unpleasant odors.

In March 1983, a Los Peñasquitos Lagoon Enhancement Program began operation through cooperation of the California Coastal Commission and the Coastal Conservancy with assistance from the newly formed (and Conservancy approved) Los Peñasquitos Lagoon Foundation. Members of the Foundation board represent the State, City of San Diego, and San Diego County administration, as well as land developers and private environmental groups. The collection of an impact fee from applicants for building permits within Los Peñasquitos watershed, as a mitigation measure, had resulted in the state policy for protection and restoration of the lagoon and wetlands. In March 1985, the planned restoration was announced in the Los Peñasquitos Lagoon Enhancement Plan, a guidebook approved for implementation of state restoration policy.

The planned program has proceeded so that tidal action approaches the stated goals, with more extensive work projected into the future. Wetland acquisition has been achieved through state purchase of the 200+ acres of former San Diego Gas & Electric utility land which encompasses major lagoon channels into Torrey Pines State Reserve. Other additions to the south include approximately 20 acres of valuable wetland in Sorrento Valley. Stewardship has been accepted for the 22-acre open space easement that extends from the Torrey Pines Extension to the lagoon below, south of Carmel Valley Road.

The Foundation continues in its main function which is to keep the lagoon mouth open, monitor physical changes, restore habitat, and improve channel circulation.

In a geological sense, all lagoons are ephemeral because the filling-in of the marshlands and channels eventually leads to their conversion to dry land. The rate at which this filling process occurs, however, depends largely on the rate of silt deposition and accumulation of organic material in the lagoon. Los Peñasquitos Lagoon will not escape this ultimate fate, but a long remaining life-span will depend on the foresight of the present generation of citizens who will determine whether this life span will be measured in thousands of years or merely a few decades.

SEAWEED DRIFT

On the sandy beaches below the cliffs at Torrey Pines there are few rocky surfaces to which marine plants, either seagrasses or seaweeds, can attach. The rocks in the intertidal region are mostly rather flat and covered during many months of the year by sand, so that those plants that are able to grow here need to be able to persist despite sand abrasion and partial burial, or to be "weedy," fast-growing species that can utilize the rock surfaces when they are exposed for a few months at a time. Higher on the beach, when rocks are free from sand, one finds mats of soft red, golden-brown, or green filaments which are different kinds of algae. Closer to the low-tide line, the algal turf will be thicker, with various low-growing branched forms, mostly purplish-black or pale lavender-pink. These latter have calcium carbonate deposited in the walls and feel different from non-calcified algae. Many years ago they were considered related to coral, and still are referred to as 'coralline' algae. After several days of day-time low tides during winter months, when the rocks along the beach have been exposed to bright light and dry air for many hours, the coralline plants bleach to pale pink or white, die, and are broken and washed away by surf. In the lowest region that is exposed by low tides are some flat rocks covered with bright green surf-grass, *Phyllospadix torreyi*, with narrow leaves that can be up to a meter or more long. Several species of seaweeds are associated with patches of *Phyllospadix* but live hidden beneath the layer of leaves that keeps them moist and cool during low tides.

Walking along the beach, particularly after periods of either summer or winter high surf, other kinds of marine plants can be found cast up, carried onto the beach from offshore deeper water sites. Most common are bits and pieces of Giant Kelp (*Macrocystis*), which grows in large beds between Pt. Loma and Del Mar. Often the large holdfasts with many attached stalks (stipes) each bearing regularly spaced blades, will be washed up on the beach. At other times, only fragments of these stalks, or separate blades each with a small oval bladder (float) at the base where it attaches to the stalk, will be scattered across the beach. Two other species of large brown seaweeds grow offshore and can be broken loose and washed up onto the sand by storms: Feather Boa Kelp (*Egregia*) resembles a flat belt fringed with blades and floats, while Southern Elk Kelp (*Pelagophycus*) has single huge floats each with a pair of attached antler-like branches. These branches are usually broken by the time they end up on the beach, but when the float is attached to the long stalk that grows up from the bottom in water 20-30 m deep, huge blades hang suspended from the branches that grow from either side of the float.

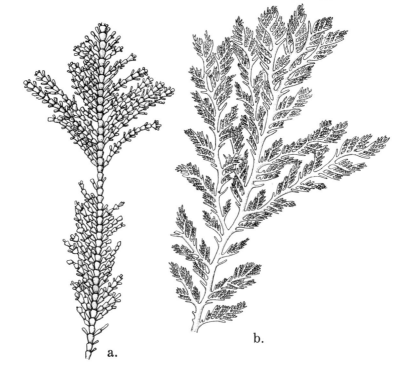

Figure 24–*Seaweeds*

    a.   *A coralline alga.*

    b.   *An example of the small, brightly colored, finely branched red algae.*

Many kinds of small red, purple, or brownish algae are washed ashore during periods of rough water or strong waves, but no single species is usually very abundant on the beach, and will vary from season to season. Two species of *Sargassum* are conspicuous when they are present, and *Pterocladia capillacea* and *Gelidium robustum* are larger and more easily recognized than the other, more delicate forms. When clumps of *Phyllospadix* are broken away from the rocks where they grow, they can be found on the beach, often with small pale pink blades or tendrils or a reddish alga growing attached to the long strands of green leaves. Even without a microscope, you can see different kinds of branching patterns, many shades of the three basic red, green and brown colors, and if you visit at various times during the year, it will be possible to discriminate amongst some of the 50-60 species of marine algae that grow in submerged habitats, but that can be found in beach drift.

INVERTEBRATES

Many kinds of "animals without backbones" may be found along and near the ocean shore of the Reserve. On the sand beaches, between tidal limits, one encounters a number of species feeding on the cast-up kelp. Among these, seaweed flies and kelp flies abound, along with semiterrestrial marine forms, such as the sandfleas, which are species of amphipod crustaceans that wildly hop about when one overturns a batch of stranded kelp, but quickly disappear in the moist sand. Sand crabs, which when soft (recently molted) are often used as bait, abound in the wet sand in the surge belt of the waves, making little triangular ripples as they expose their appendages to catch food as the wave recedes.

The intertidal sandy beach is the home of the little wedge-shaped Bean Clam that at times occurs in enormous numbers. Pismo Clams (generally under legal size) also live in the sand and surf zone. Conspicuous here also are groups of the burrowing sand crabs and the numerous burrowing worms and smaller crustaceans. In the rocky intertidal area are found California Mussels, Limpets, Shore Crabs, several barnacles, and many other invertebrates.

The bottom offshore, especially on rock bottom and among seaweeds (algae and surfgrass), harbors a great variety of invertebrate animals. Some of these are to be seen washed up dead or alive on the sandy beach. Among the most conspicuous of these are Sand-dollars, along with various kinds of clams and snails (among which the Wavy Topshell attracts attention).

Other invertebrates come ashore in large numbers in the stranded holdfasts ("roots") of the Giant Kelp, the Southern Elk Kelp and the Feather Boa Kelp. In addition to many worms and small crustaceans the holdfasts harbor brittle-stars, sea-urchins, delicate Broad-eared Scallops and young Red Abalone.

Several of the species mentioned above are illustrated on Figure 23.

THE OCEAN

The waters in the Torrey Pines State Reserve, and in the immediately adjacent ocean, harbor a wealth of aquatic life, all of which is of value to scientists and much of which is of interest to the more casual visitor. Aquatic birds are conspicuous members of the aquatic fauna of the Reserve, but are treated elsewhere in this booklet.

Only a few of the most conspicuous of the many animals of the adjacent ocean can be noted here. Hundreds of species live in the varied oceanic habitats in and close to the Reserve: along the sand and pebbly beaches, on the limited intertidal rock exposure (on Flat Rock), at the surface of the adjacent ocean, in the offshore beds of the giant kelp, and particularly on the bottom of the sea outside the surf. The ocean bottom just off the Reserve is in part a gentle sandy slope and in part a rocky shelf. The ocean bottom as well as the forests of kelp may now be observed by snorkeling, and even better by SCUBA (self-contained underwater breathing apparatus).

Marine Mammals — Most conspicuous among the local marine mammals, and among the largest, is the Gray Whale, which is most often seen as it migrates southward, often close to shore, toward the Baja California lagoons where it breeds. Locally, the numbers build up in December and the migration is in full swing through January and continues into February. The northward return is from February to April. The commonest inshore porpoise, the only one that habitually swims along shore near the surf, is the Pacific Bottlenose Porpoise, the type often seen performing in oceanaria. Occasionally seen from cliff tops of the Reserve, or stranded on a nearby beach, are the massive Sperm Whale, its little cousin the Pygmy Sperm Whale, two species of the medium-sized Beaked Whales, and four additional species of the porpoise family, including the Pilot Whale or Blackfish and the fierce Killer Whale.

The California Sea-lion is frequently seen and heard close to shore in the winter, and sick or dead ones are occasionally stranded. In close pods they often spend the night near shore. Harbor Seals sometimes appear near the surf, rearing their big-eyed, round heads out of the water.

Fishes — One of the most appealingly interesting of the marine fishes is the Grunion, which in spring and summer spawns on the moist sand, with uncanny regularity, on two to four nights after new moon and after full moon, a short time after the turn of the high tide. After both sexes are temporarily stranded by a large wave the females dig down tail-first and then deposit a ball of eggs, which are fertilized by the males as they lie on the surface. The eggs hatch out two weeks later, as they are churned out of the sand by the next series of spring tides.

Among the species caught by surf-fishing along nearby coastal areas, the Corbina is usually the most prized, though Barred Surfperch are taken in larger numbers. Other members of the viviparous (live-bearing) perch family are the Walleye Surfperch and the Black Seaperch. Yellowfin and Spotfin Croakers and, occasionally, California Halibut and Diamond Turbot are also caught from the beach. Interesting fishes which, though edible, are generally discarded by surf fishermen, are Leopard Sharks, Gray Smoothhounds, Shovelnose Guitarfish, Round Stingrays (which at times inflict painful wounds on the feet of surf bathers who do not take pains to shuffle along), and, less commonly, the much larger Bat Ray.

Other kinds of fish are caught from boats offshore, but they are beyond the scope of this booklet.

PREHISTORIC PEOPLES IN
TORREY PINES STATE RESERVE

Between 8,000 and 9,000 years ago, hunting peoples from the interior valleys of California began moving into the southern coastal region. Perhaps they were retreating from the increasingly drier environment following the end of the Pleistocene, or perhaps they were drawn to the teeming lagoons and estuaries that had formed with rising sea level. Numerous shell middens dating from 8,300 to 2,000 years old are scattered along the high sea cliffs stretching from Torrey Pines State Reserve south to La Jolla. During these six millennia, the prehistoric people now known as the La Jollans relied on plant food gathering and collecting of shellfish and other littoral resources. Artifacts from their occupation sites consist of basin-shaped milling stones (metates and manos), flakes, scrapers, quantities of broken, fire-altered stones, very few projectile points, and occasional perforated or cog-shaped stones. Bone and shell artifacts are sometimes preserved and may have been awls, needles and fishhooks. Many of these sites contain flexed burials. Some are interred beneath inverted metates; others have grave goods such as shell beads and ornaments.

Prehistoric sites are found within the Reserve both along the mesa top and along the shores of Los Peñasquitos Lagoon. During La Jollan times, the lagoons of San Diego County were deep, open to the ocean and flushed with salt water, forming ideal habitats for many varieties of shellfish and spawning grounds for marine fish.

Excavations at one of the shell middens on the mesa indicate that the people who camped there hunted and collected shellfish from the rocky, exposed seacoast and from the protected lagoon waters to the east. Radiocarbon dates of around 5,000 years B.P. (before present) place this site in mid-La Jollan times.

Offshore, artifacts have been found at many localities along the San Diego County coast. Circular cobble grinding stones called mortars occur by the hundreds at the southern head of Scripps Submarine Canyon off La Jolla Shores, and have been sighted in the nearshore rocky reef south of Flat Rock in the Reserve. At depths of 3 to 5 meters, they may be remnants of manufacturing sites along the cobble beach of circa 5,000 years ago. As mortars are found almost exclusively in submarine localities off the San Diego County coast, they seemingly had some function in littoral collecting or kelp-bed fishing activities. Seafaring capability even in the early stages of coastal occupation is demonstrated by radiocarbon dates of 8,000 years B.P. from San Clemente and Santa Rosa Islands.

The La Jollans who lived along these sea cliffs during the warm, dry centuries of the mid-Holocene found a rocky, productive littoral zone for collecting molluscs and fishing. Rafts or canoes were probably used to fish the kelp beds off Point La Jolla and Torrey Pines State Reserve. Nearby lagoons at Los Peñasquitos and possibly La Jolla Shores offered molluscs, fish, waterbirds, and plant resources. Hunting of small mammals and plant food gathering within the riparian habitats of the stream valleys above the lagoons contributed to a diversified diet which sustained these populations over a period of 6,000 years on the Southern California coast.

Appearing in the upper levels of archaeological sites and dating back to 1,500 years ago, a different culture called the Diegueño or Kumeyaay replaced the La Jollan. It is not known if this transition represents a new migration of people from the desert areas to the east or if it merely reflects diffusion of cultural traits. These late-prehistoric people made pottery and cremated their dead, but like the La Jollans they pursued a diversified littoral-terrestrial collecting economy.

At the time of Spanish contact, the Kumeyaay of coastal San Diego County participated in an extensive trade network reaching from the Arizona desert and central valley of California to the Channel Islands and south into Baja California. In addition to collecting molluscs, they built tule rafts and canoes for fishing the lagoons and nearshore waters. Game animals included rabbits, hares, squirrels, rats, and birds. They gathered grasses, seeds, and acorns. Along with other native peoples, they set brush fires to drive game and to encourage new growth of tender grasses for food. Consequently, the Kumeyaay were generally healthy and well-fed due to a seasonal round of utilization of local resources, some environmental manipulation, and exploiting the diversity of native foodstuffs to be found within ecotones (intersection of two or more ecological zones). Torrey Pines State Reserve and nearby valleys were home to coastal Kumeyaay groups, and a village called Ystagua existed in Sorrento Valley.

Fortunately, most of these sites of pre-Spanish occupation remain relatively undisturbed in spite of the thousands of people visiting the Reserve. The preservation of these scientific treasures is attributable to the rugged terrain, dense brush and enforcement of laws prohibiting vandalism and the removal of any object. If you see an Indian relic, please let it remain in place!

GEOLOGY OF TORREY PINES
STATE RESERVE

Torrey Pines State Reserve is as remarkable for its geological as for its biological features. Extensive sea-cliff and canyon-wall exposures reveal several unusually interesting bedrock formations as well as an exceptional sequence of younger shoreline marine features and faults of the Rose Canyon zone.

The bedrock formations are the result of sediments laid down in seas that covered this region during the mid-Eocene epoch, some 45 million years ago. The various kinds of Eocene rocks record a complex pattern of marine environmental settings which shifted back and forth across the area of the present coastal zone: the outcrops are of great interest to geologists from around the world.

Notched into and overlying the bedrock formations is a series of uplifted marine terraces which formed during the past several hundred thousand years of the Pleistocene. These provide a remarkable record of the interplay between fluctuating world-wide sea levels and changing levels of land. During this time a system of faults also developed which cut through the bedrock formations and the older terraces at the Reserve.

EOCENE ROCKS

At least nine separate rock formations distinguished by composition, texture and color, record geologic events during the middle part of the Eocene Epoch in San Diego. Three of them are exposed in Torrey Pines State Reserve. Until the 1970's these rock units were interpreted as being stacked regularly one atop another like layers of a cake. Then interfingering relationships were found, and it was suggested that a series of marine environments had shifted back and forth as sea level fluctuated, in some areas spreading formations across the tops of nearby layers with which they were contemporaneous.

In the Reserve's central area and in the Extension north of the lagoon, the bedrock units are the Del Mar Formation and the partly younger, partly contemporaneous Torrey Sandstone (Figure 25). The former is the gray-green muddy sandstone exposed in the lower half of the sea cliffs as far south as Flat Rock. The Torrey Sandstone is the yellow-white or buff-colored rock that occupies the upper half of the sea cliffs and all the higher ground, below the Pleistocene terraces, both in the central area of the Reserve and the northern Extension. Both formations extend north and east as far as Carlsbad and Rancho Santa Fe. Interfingering relationships, which suggest that adjacent parts of these two formations were deposited in different environments at the same time, can be seen in the Reserve's sea-cliff exposures.

The fossil oyster beds that are so prominent in the Del Mar Formation indicate deposition in protected bays, lagoons, or estuaries. A variety of other fossil clams and snails occur with the oysters and also in adjacent beds throughout the formation. Abundant fossil burrows excavated by molluscs, crabs, annelid worms, and other invertebrates are also present, especially in muds directly below the oyster beds. They record an even greater richness of life than that indicated by the shelly fossils alone. Sandier beds with ripple marks and cross-strata apparently were deposited on tidal flats and in tidal and subtidal channels and ponds within the embayments.

The Torrey Sandstone consists of cross-bedded lenses up to 4 meters deep and 30 meters wide where sand was deposited in underwater dunes or in channels associated with a tidal delta or with offshore barrier bars. Fossil shells are rare in these rocks, but a variety of fossil burrows attest to the former abundance of marine invertebrates.

Southward from Flat Rock (which is a resistant bed in the Del Mar Formation) the sea cliffs are cut in the roughly contemporaneous Ardath Shale and in associated pebbly sandstones. The latter were deposited in the head of a submarine canyon, in water depths of a few hundred meters. The base of these beds is marked by a layer of angular mudstone boulders which are conspicuous in the sea cliff at Flat Rock and along the Beach Trail at the top of that cliff.

Southward along the beach one walks deeper into the Ardath Shale. These fine-grained rocks originated as muddy sediments deposited in a submarine canyon cut into the continental slope farther offshore. Much of this part of the formation consists of deposits in channels up to 600 meters wide and 75 meters deep. Channels were eroded repeatedly in the floor of the submarine canyon, then filled with sediment swept off the shelf above. Fossil foraminifera indicate that these channels were eroded and filled between the shelf edge and the base of the continental slope, in water depths from 200 to 1500 meters. Increasing depths are recorded by rocks to the south, in the area near the glider port, where the channels become even more prominent.

Figure 25—*Gull's-eye view, from the west, of geologic features at Torrey Pines State Reserve. Non-marine terrace deposits are stippled, and their basal marine layers are shown as lines of boulders. Heavy lines are faults.*

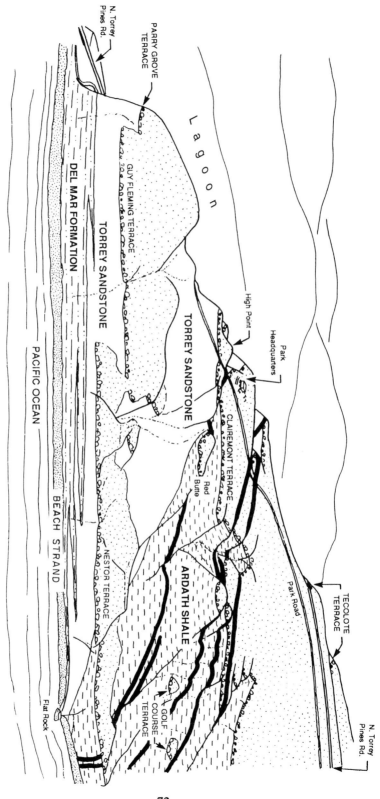

73

Thus a southward walk along the sea cliffs of Torrey Pines State Reserve takes one through a series of bedrock formations that originated under increasingly deep-water marine conditions. It is this remarkable cross-section view of the fluctuating environments of mid-Eocene seas that draws geologists to the area.

PLEISTOCENE MARINE SHORELINES

During the past million years sea level has risen and fallen repeatedly in response to alternate advance and retreat of continental glaciers and corresponding changes in the volume of water locked up on land as glacial ice. On coasts such as this which are undergoing geologic uplift at the same time, fluctuating sea levels have produced sequences of raised shorelines - wave-cut terraces, reefs, bay deposits, and lines of dunes that formed near sea level during interglacial high sea-stands but are now high and dry. Torrey Pines Reserve is notable in preserving features of at least six separate shorelines in a small area, four of them being exceptionally well exposed.

Each terrace originated as a flat, nearly horizontal platform carved into the rocky shore by waves and backed by an adjoining sea cliff. Good present-day examples are the tidepool areas at Point Loma, Sunset Cliffs, and La Jolla Bay. After being abandoned by the receding sea when the glaciers began to expand, terrace platforms are covered with sediment, usually a thin layer of wave-transported sand and rounded boulders overlain by a thick blanket of non-marine sand and mud. During the ensuing time of falling and low sea level, each terrace is gradually uplifted with the rising land, so the next high stand cuts a younger, lower shoreline bench. In time a sequence of step-like terraces is formed, the oldest at the top and the youngest at the bottom. As each terrace shoreline originated near sea level, its present elevation records the total amount of uplift that has occurred since it formed.

The oldest of the Reserve's six terraces which is exposed along its eastern boundary is the Tecolote Terrace. Only the platform's seaward edge is exposed here, at 110 meters elevation, in the steep slopes east of the crest of Torrey Pines Road and east of the ridgetop in the northern Extension. Fossil molluscs have been found on this terrace at one site in San Diego. The ratios between two structural forms of various amino acids in the protein layers of

Figure 26—*Flat Rock is a resistant sandstone bed in the Del Mar Formation. Many years ago a Welsh miner attempted to sink a shaft for a coal mine on Flat Rock. The oblong hole has given rise to many legends. It is occasionally called Bath-tub Rock. It is at the seaward end of the Beach Trail.*

those shells suggest an age for this terrace of approximately 500,000 to 600,000 years. Since the coastal zone has been raised some 110 meters above its former level during that time, and assuming sea level then and now to be the same, the average rate of uplift has been approximately 20 centimeters per thousand years.

The ridge along the Reserve's eastern boundary, clearly visible across the lagoon to the northeast from High Point or from behind the visitor center, is a former line of sand dunes that was built by the wind inland from the next younger shoreline. It is one of a number of such "beach ridges" associated with San Diego's terraces. This shoreline is that of the Clairemont terrace. It is not clearly exposed here but lies just west of the ridge in the northern Extension and along Torrey Pines Road. The terrace platform west of the shoreline, 93 meters above sea level, is clearly visible in the bank above the park road northward from High Point.

The least well preserved of the Reserve's shoreline features is a discontinuous line of very narrow benches notched into the top of the steep bluffs south of Flat Rock. Only one of these remnants is well exposed, and that one is 63 meters above sea level on a nearly inaccessible cliff-top spur isolated from the rest of the Reserve by the northern end of the Torrey Pines Golf Course. This obscure remnant of the Golf Course terrace is disproportionately important, as it is San Diego County's best exposure of a shoreline that has been almost totally destroyed by erosion.

The next younger shoreline is that of the Parry Grove terrace and it stands now at 56 meters above sea level. The sand that caps the ridgetop encircled by the Guy Fleming Trail and the sea-facing slopes above the Parry Grove Trail was blown into dunes here on top of this terrace. The only moderately clear view of its platform is in the north wall of the Canyon of the Swifts. An inconspicuous foot-thick horizontal bed of sea-rounded pebbles up to a few inches in diameter is visible at about eye level across the canyon from the second overlook platform on the Razor Point Trail.

From the same vantage point one can also see the next lower shoreline, that of the Guy Fleming terrace. On the face of the slope to the left, 46 meters above sea level and 10 meters below the higher platform, a second band of rounded stones extends northward. This terrace can also be seen from afar by looking southward from the far north end of the beach opposite the lagoon. Look for the distinct horizontal line marked by a color change from yellow-white sandstone of the vertical cliffs to darker brown sand in the slopes above.

Figure 27–*View seaward along upper part of Great Basin showing flat top of Nestor terrace sloping gently seaward. The dark, fluted terrace deposits rest on light-colored, massive Torrey Sandstone.*

This terrace platform thus lies somewhat below and parallel to the seaward half of the loop of the Guy Fleming Trail.

The Nestor terrace is most conspicuous as it stretches along nearly the entire coastline. From the adjacent beach it is clearly visible where a horizontal layer of wave-rounded boulders and sand overlies resistant bedrock some 15 to 18 meters up the cliff face. Look for it from just south of Flat Rock northward for a quarter of a mile. In places the basal layer of sea-deposited sand and boulders is covered by a thick blanket of featureless dark brown muddy sand that was washed onto it later by erosion from the higher slopes.

The Nestor terrace is the only one within the Reserve that bears fossil shells. They can be seen along the lower end of the Broken Hill Trail near its junction with the Beach Trail. The fossils, including abundant Pismo clams, bean clams, olive shells, limpets, mussels, and oysters, are characteristic of both sandy and rocky environments, and nearly all the fossil species can be found living today just off the modern beach. The terrace shoreline is 23 meters above present sea level, showing that the land has been uplifted some 17 meters here (this terrace was carved 120,000 years ago during the sea-stand approximately 6 meters higher than the present one). The average rate of uplift during this time, then, is only about 14 centimeters each thousand years. The age of this terrace was determined by the more reliable technique of radiometric dating, which is based on precisely measured ratios between radioactive isotopes and the daughter isotopes into which they decay at known rates. The Nestor terrace is conspicuous at about this elevation at the Mexican border, Point Loma, and Pacific Beach, and it is somewhat higher under downtown La Jolla, where it has been uplifted along the Rose Canyon fault.

A possible seventh and still younger shoreline has no wave-cut terrace here but may be represented by the flat-topped bench just east of Torrey Pines Road at the southwestern corner of the lagoon. This is an alluvial fan that appears to have been graded to a sea level some five meters or so higher than the present one.

PLEISTOCENE FAULTS

Both the bedrock formations and several of the older terraces are cut by northeast-trending faults of the Rose Canyon zone. The Rose Canyon fault itself, which passes just offshore in a north-northwesterly direction, is active and

Figure 28—Erosion is one of the powerful forces in shaping the beauty of this area. View of the north wall of the Canyon of the Swifts showing Torrey Sandstone with typical light color, massive structure and hollows caused by weathering.

may be a source of future earthquakes. Though relationships with the younger terraces cannot be seen at Torrey Pines Reserve, it is clear elsewhere that the northeastward-trending branch faults do not cut the Nestor terrace, and thus that they have not moved for at least 120,000 years. They do cut the older terraces, though, as one can see in the canyons heading behind the Reserve's visitor center.

From High Point, or from the road between there and the visitor center, the Clairemont terrace can be seen as a red-brown layer of sand and gravel capping the white sandstone ridge a few meters to the east. Look across to the cliff face behind the visitor center and you will see that the base of the red-brown terrace sand extends some nine meters into the canyon. The prominent difference across the canyon in thickness of red-brown beds, together with the presence of the High Point ridge of sand on just one side, shows that rocks on opposite sides of the fault, which lies in the bed of the canyon, have moved past one another mostly in a horizontal direction. In other words, it is a strike-slip fault, as are its companions in the Reserve and the Rose Canyon fault itself.

From here this fault passes into the head of the canyon west of the road, crosses the swale east of Red Butte, and then runs diagonally down to the shore. There it is clearly visible as a prominent pair of fractures in the sea-cliff rocks 100 meters south of Flat Rock. Other faults are equally well exposed in the cliffs further to the south. One of these faults can also be seen an eighth of a mile south of the visitor center, in the uppermost canyon wall immediately to the east of the Reserve road.

The story related here is incomplete. Within the Reserve there is no record of what happened between the deposition of Eocene sediments around 45 million years ago and the cutting of the terraces beginning less than a million years ago. Between San Diego and the Orange County/Los Angeles area there are, however, strata which contain an almost continuous record of these, and even earlier millennia but none of these rocks has been preserved in the Torrey Pines Reserve area.

The raised marine terraces in the Reserve record the interplay of two totally independent natural processes. The rise and fall of sea level was driven by climatic changes, the uplift of the land by movements deep within the earth's crust. Such a delicate record of the combined effects of these two wholly different variables is not common, a fact that enhances the value of the Reserve.

Figure 29—*Torrey Pines cliffs from the beach, with La Jolla in the distance. The lower half is part of the Del Mar Formation overlain by Torrey Sandstone and a thin layer of terrace deposits.*

What will the future bring? Modern measurements indicate that sea level has risen about 17.5cm in the past 100 years and some scientists project that a significant rise may take place in the next century or two as a result of global warming induced by man's contribution to the "Greenhouse Effect." If this happens it will probably be the first time in earth's 4-plus billion year history that life on earth has deliberately and significantly interfered with the normally self-correcting balance of processes that sustain our environment.

CONCLUSION

The citizens of San Diego and the State of California are fortunate to have within their boundaries Torrey Pines State Reserve, a fascinating bit of the past, that must be protected for all time from reckless exploitation and despoliation. It forms a natural exhibit that cannot be excelled or duplicated in any other portion of the world. It is a priceless heritage; let us all help to preserve its beauty for generations to come.

> Do not permit the love of plants and the zeal of the collector to make this into a botanical garden or plant museum which will leave no semblance to the original landscape. Do not introduce features or plants foreign to the spirit and feeling of this area as it now exists. . . . Remember that Torrey Pines' fame was won without man's creative aid and that preservation rather than change should be sought.
>
> Ralph D. Cornell - 1922

REFERENCES

Balls, Edward K. 1972. Early Uses of California Plants. California Natural History Guides No. 10. University of California Press, Berkeley.

Beauchamp, R. Mitchel. 1986. Flora of San Diego County. Sweetwater River Press, National City, CA.

Booth, Ernest S. 1986. Mammals of Southern California. California Natural History Guides No. 21. University of California Press, Berkeley.

Carrico, Richard L. 1987. Strangers in a Stolen Land; American Indians in San Diego, 1650-1880. Sierra Oaks Pub., Sacramento.

Chapman, T. 1973. See the Forest for the Trees. Torrey Pines Association, La Jolla.

Coles, D. Shane. 1983. The Ethnobotany of Torrey Pines State Reserve. California State Department of Parks and Recreation, Sacramento.

Dale, Nancy. 1986. Flowering Plants: the Santa Monica Mountains, Coastal and Chaparral Regions of Southern California. Capra Press, Santa Barbara, CA.

Eschmeyer, William N., Earl S. Herald, and Howard Hamman. 1983. A Field Guide to Pacific Coast Fishes of North America. Houghton Mifflin Co., Boston.

Hinton, Sam. 1987. Seashore Life of Southern California: An Introduction to the Animal Life of California Beaches South of Santa Barbara. California Natural History Guides No. 26. University of California Press, Berkeley.

Kennedy, Michael P., and Gary L. Peterson. 1975. Geology of the San Diego Metropolitan Area, California. California Division of Mines and Geology Bulletin 200.

Kuhn, Gerald G., and Francis P. Shepard. 1984. Sea Cliffs, Beaches and Coastal Valleys of San Diego County: Some Amazing Histories and Some Horrifying Implications. University of California Press, Berkeley.

Munz, Philip A. 1961. California Spring Wildflowers from the Base of the Sierra Nevada and Southern Mountains to the Sea. University of California Press, Berkeley.

_____. 1962. California Desert Wildflowers. University of California Press, Berkeley.

_____. 1963. California Mountain Wildflowers. University of California Press, Berkeley.

_____. 1964. Shore Wildflowers of California, Oregon and Washington. University of California Press, Berkeley.

Figure 30–*The old Torrey Pines Lodge, which now serves as State Reserve headquarters. The Torrey Pines in the background were planted in 1923.*

Munz, Philip A. 1974. A Flora of Southern California. University of California Press, Berkeley.

National Geographic Society. 1988. Field Guide to the Birds of North America. Second Ed. The Society, Washington, D.C.

Nicol, Donald W. 1981. Notes from the Naturalist. Torrey Pines Docent Society, San Diego.

_____. 1985. Torrey Pines: Beyond the Trees. Torrey Pines Docent Society, San Diego.

Peterson, Peter V. 1966. Native Trees of Southern California. California Natural History Guides No. 14. University of California Press, Berkeley.

Peterson, Roger T. 1984. Birds of the American West: A Field Guide to Western Birds. Peterson Field Guide Series. Easton Press, Norwalk, CT.

Powell, Jerry A., and Charles L. Hogue. 1979. California Insects. California Natural History Guides No. 44. University of California Press, Berkeley.

Raven, Peter R. 1970. Native Shrubs of Southern California. California Natural History Guides No. 15. University of California Press, Berkeley.

Ricketts, Edward F., Jack Calvin, and Joel W. Hedgpeth. 1985. Between Pacific Tides. Fifth Ed. Stanford University Press, Stanford.

Robbins, Chandler S., Bertel Bruun, and Herbert S. Zim. 1986. Birds of North America: A Guide to Field Identification. Revised Ed. Golden Press, New York.

Stebbins, Robert C. 1985. A Field Guide to Western Reptiles and Amphibians. Second Ed. Peterson Field Guide Series No. 16. Houghton Mifflin, Boston.

Unitt, Philip. 1984. The Birds of San Diego County. San Diego Natural History Museum, San Diego.

Witham, Helen. 1972. Ferns of San Diego County. San Diego Natural History Museum, San Diego, CA.

APPENDIX

PLANTS AND ANIMALS OF THE TORREY PINES RESERVE

PLANTS	* = Non-native Taxa
Common Name	**Scientific Name**

ALGAE
  PHAEOPHYTA - BROWN ALGAE
    Giant Kelp — *Macrocystis pyrifera*
    Elk Kelp — *Pelagophycus porra*
    Feather Boa Kelp — *Egregia laevigata*
  RHODOPHYTA - RED ALGAE
    Finely-branched Red Alga — *Plocamium pacificum*
    Coralline Alga — *Corallina officinalis*
  CHLOROPHYTA - GREEN ALGAE
    Sea Lettuce — *Ulva* sp.
    Sea Felt — *Enteromorpha* spp.

FERNS
  POLYPODIACEAE
    California Maidenhair — *Adiantum jordani*
    Coffee Fern — *Pellaea andromedifolia*
    Bird's Foot Cliff-Brake — *Pellaea mucronata*
    Silverback Fern — *Pityrogramma triangularis* var. *viscosa*
    Coastal Woodfern — *Dryopteris arguta*
    California Polypody — *Polypodium californicum*

GYMNOSPERMS
  CUPRESSACEAE - CYPRESS FAMILY
    * Monterey Cypress — *Cupressus macrocarpa*
  PINACEAE - PINE FAMILY
    Torrey Pine — *Pinus torreyana* var. *torreyana*

FLOWERING PLANTS - DICOTYLEDONS
  ADOXACEAE - ADOXUS FAMILY
    Desert Elderberry — *Sambucus mexicana*
  AIZOACEAE - CARPET-WEED FAMILY
    * Sea-Fig — *Carpobrotus aequilaterus*
    * — *Carpobrotus aequilaterus* X *edulis*
    * Hottentot-Fig — *Carpobrotus edulis*
    * Lampranthus — *Lampranthus coccineus*
    * Crystal Ice Plant — *Mesembryanthemum crystallinum*
    * Little Ice Plant — *Mesembryanthemum nodiflorum*
    * New Zealand-Spinach — *Tetragonia tetragonioides*
  AMARANTHACEAE - AMARANTH FAMILY
    Pigweed — *Amaranthus blitoides*
  ANACARDIACEAE - SUMAC FAMILY
    Laurel-Leaf Sumac — *Malosma laurina*
    Lemonade Berry — *Rhus integrifolia*
    Sugarbush — *Rhus ovata*
    Basketbush — *Rhus trilobata* var. *quinata*
    * Pepper-tree — *Schinus molle*
    Poison-Oak — *Toxicodendron radicans* ssp. *diversilobum*

APIACEAE - CARROT FAMILY
  Wild-celery — *Apiastrum angustifolium*
* Celery — *Apium graveolens*
  Bowlesia — *Bowlesia incana*
* Poison-Hemlock — *Conium maculatum*
  Rattlesnake Weed — *Daucus pusillus*
* Sweet Fennel — *Foeniculum vulgare*
  — *Lomatium lucidum*
  Sanicle — *Sanicula bipinnatifolia*
  — *Sanicula crassicaulis*

ASCLEPIADACEAE - MILKWEED FAMILY
  Hartweg's Milkvine — *Sarcostemma cynanchoides* ssp. *hartwegii*

ASTERACEAE - SUNFLOWER FAMILY
  Yarrow — *Achillea millefolium* var. *californica*
  Sacapellote, Purpleheads — *Acourtia microcephala*
  Bather's Delight — *Ambrosia bipinnatifida*
  Western Ragweed — *Ambrosia psilostachya* var. *californica*
  Pineapple Weed — *Amblyopappus pusillus*
  California Sagebrush — *Artemisia californica*
  Dragon Sagewort — *Artemisia dracunculus*
  San Diego Sagewort — *Artemisia palmeri*
  Emory's Baccharis — *Baccharis emoryi*
  Coyote Brush — *Baccharis pilularis* ssp. *consanguinea*
  Mule-fat — *Baccharis salicifolia*
  Broom Baccharis — *Baccharis sarothroides*
  Rosinweed — *Calycadenia tenella*
* Tocalote — *Centaurea melitensis*
  Pincushion — *Chaenactis artemisiaefolia*
  San Diego Pincushion — *Chaenactis glabriuscula* var. *tenuifolia*
* Garland Chrysanthemum — *Chrysanthemum coronarium*
  Golden-Aster — *Chrysopsis villosa*
  California Thistle — *Cirsium californicum*
  Cobweb Thistle — *Cirsium occidentale*
* Flax-Leaf Fleabane — *Conyza bonariensis*
* Horseweed — *Conyza canadensis*
  San Diego Sea-Dahlia — *Coreopsis maritima*
  Del Mar Sand-aster — *Corethrogyne filaginifolia* var. *linifolia*
  Virgate Cudweed-Aster — *Corethrogyne filaginifolia* var. *virgata*
* Australian Brass-Buttons — *Cotula australis*
* Brass-Buttons — *Cotula coronopifolia*
  California Encelia — *Encelia californica*
* Brittle-Bush — *Encelia farinosa*
  Leaf Daisy — *Erigeron foliosus* var. *foliosus*
  Golden-Yarrow — *Eriophyllum confertiflorum* var. *confertiflorum*
  Filago — *Filago californica*
  Fragrant Everlasting — *Gnaphalium beneolens*
  Bicolor Cudweed — *Gnaphalium bicolor*
  California Everlasting — *Gnaphalium californicum*
  Everlasting — *Gnaphalium microcephalum*
  Sawtooth Goldenbush — *Hazardia squarrosa* ssp. *grindelioides*
* Crete Hedypnois — *Hedypnois cretica*

PLANTS (CONTINUED)	* = Non-native Taxa
Common Name	**Scientific Name**

ASTERACEAE - SUNFLOWER FAMILY (continued)

*	Western Sunflower	*Helianthus annuus* ssp. *lenticularis*
	Fascicled Tarweed	*Hemizonia fasciculata*
	Telegraph Weed	*Heterotheca grandiflora*
*	Smooth Cat's-ears	*Hypochoeris glabra*
	Coastal Goldenbush	*Isocoma menziesii* var. *vernonioides*
	Western Marsh Elder	*Iva axillaris* ssp. *robusitor*
	San Diego Marsh-Elder	*Iva hayesiana*
	Salty Susan	*Jaumea carnosa*
*	Prickly Lettuce	*Lactuca serriola*
	Goldfields	*Lasthenia californica*
	Southern Goldfields	*Lasthenia coronaria*
	Coulter's Saltmarsh-Daisy	*Lasthenia glabrata* ssp. *coulteri*
	Common Tidy-tips	*Layia platyglossa* ssp. *campestris*
	Silver Puffs	*Microseris lindleyi*
	Marsh Fleabane	*Pluchea odorata*
	California Chicory	*Rafinesquia californica*
	California Butterweed	*Senecio californicus*
*	Common Groundsel	*Senecio vulgaris*
*	Spiny-Leaf Sow-Thistle	*Sonchus asper*
*	Common Sow-Thistle	*Sonchus oleraceus*
	San Diego Wreath-Plant	*Stephanomeria diegensis*
	Virgate Wreath-Plant	*Stephanomeria virgata* ssp. *virgata*
	Everlasting Nest-Straw	*Stylocline gnaphalioides*
	Arrowweed	*Tessaria sericea*
*	Cocklebur	*Xanthium strumarium*

BERBERIDACEAE - BARBERRY FAMILY

*	Nevin's Mahonia	*Mahonia nevinii*

BORAGINACEAE - BORAGE FAMILY

Rancher's Fiddleneck	*Amsinckia intermedia*
Nievitas	*Cryptantha intermedia*
Heliotrope	*Heliotropium curvassavicum*
California Popcornflower	*Plagiobothrys californicus* var. *californicus*
	Plagiobothrys trachycarpus

BRASSICACEAE - MUSTARD FAMILY

*	Short-pod Mustard	*Brassica geniculata*
*	Black Mustard	*Brassica nigra*
*	Sea-Rocket	*Cakile edentula*
	Milkmaids	*Cardamine californica*
	Western Tansy-Mustard	*Descurainia pinata* ssp. *halietorum*
	Draba	*Draba cuneifolia* var. *cuneifolia*
	Western Wallflower	*Erysimum capitatum*
	Prostrate Hutchinsia	*Hutchinsia procumbens*
	Robinson's Peppergrass	*Lepidium virginicum* var. *robinsonii*
*	Sweet Alyssum	*Lobularia maritima*
*	Common Stock	*Matthiola incana*
*	Wild Radish	*Raphanus sativus*
*	Tumble-Mustard	*Sisymbrium altissimum*
*	London Rocket	*Sisymbrium irio*

BRASSICACEAE - MUSTARD FAMILY (continued)
* Hedge Mustard — *Sisymbrium orientale*
  San Diego Jewelflower — *Streptanthus heterophyllus*
BUXACEAE - JOJOBA FAMILY
  Jojoba — *Simmondsia chinensis*
CACTACEAE - CACTUS FAMILY
* Golden Snake-Cactus — *Bergerocactus emoryi*
  Coast Barrel Cactus — *Ferocactus viridescens*
  Fish-hook Cactus — *Mammillaria dioica*
  Coast Prickly-Pear — *Opuntia littoralis* var. *littoralis*
  Western Prickly-Pear — *Opuntia occidentalis*
  Coast Cholla — *Opuntia prolifera*
CAPPARACEAE - CAPER FAMILY
  Bladderpod — *Cleome isomeris*
CAPRIFOLIACEAE - HONEYSUCKLE FAMILY
  San Diego Honeysuckle — *Lonicera subspicata* var. *denudata*
CARYOPHYLLACEAE - PINK FAMILY
  Tread Lightly — *Cardionema ramosissima*
  Mouse-Ear Chickweed — *Cerastium glomeratum*
  California Polycarp — *Polycarpon depressum*
* Four-Leaf Polycarp — *Polycarpon tetraphyllum*
  Snapdragon Catchfly — *Silene antirrhina*
* Common Catchfly — *Silene gallica*
  Large-Flower Sand-Spurry — *Spergularia macrotheca* var. *leucantha*
* La Plata Sand-Spurry — *Spergularia platensis*
* Salt Marsh Sand-Spurry — *Spergularia marina*
  Villous Sand-Spurry — *Spergularia villosa*
* Chickweed — *Stellaria media*
CHENOPODIACEAE - GOOSEFOOT FAMILY
  Aphanisma — *Aphanisma blitoides*
  Four-wing Saltbush — *Atriplex canescens* ssp. *canescens*
  Quail Saltbush — *Atriplex lentiformis*
  Seascale — *Atriplex leucophylla*
  Halberd-Leaf Saltbush — *Atriplex patula* ssp. *hastata*
* Australian Saltbush — *Atriplex semibaccata*
* Five-hook Bassia — *Bassia hyssopifolia*
* Lamb's Quarters — *Chenopodium album*
* Mexican-Tea — *Chenopodium ambrosioides*
  California Goosefoot — *Chenopodium californicum*
* Nettle-Leaf Goosefoot — *Chenopodium murale*
* Goosefoot — *Chenopodium* sp.
  Slender Glasswort — *Salicornia europaea*
  Parish's Glasswort — *Salicornia subterminalis*
  Pickleweed — *Salicornia virginica*
* Russian-thistle — *Salsola australis*
  Sea-Blite — *Suaeda californica* var. *pubescens*
CISTACEAE - ROCK-ROSE FAMILY
  Rush-Rose — *Helianthemum scoparium* var. *aldersonii*

90

CONVOLVULACEAE - MORNING-GLORY FAMILY

Common Name	Scientific Name
Morning-Glory	*Calystegia macrostegia* ssp. *longiloba*
Narrow-leaf Morning-Glory	*Calystegia macrostegia* ssp. *tenuifolia*
* Field Bindweed	*Convolvulus arvensis*
Alkali Weed	*Cressa truxillensis* var. *vallicola*
Witch's Hair	*Cuscuta californica*
Salt Marsh Dodder	*Cuscuta salina*
Western Ponyfoot	*Dichondra occidentalis*

CRASSULACEAE - STONECROP FAMILY

Common Name	Scientific Name
Del Mar Hasseanthus	*Dudleya brevifolia*
Dwarf Stonecrop	*Crassula connata* var. *connata*
Ladies-Fingers	*Dudleya edulis*
Coastal Dudleya	*Dudleya lanceolata*
Chalk-lettuce	*Dudleya pulverulenta*
San Diego Hasseanthus	*Dudleya variegata*

CUCURBITACEAE - GOURD FAMILY

Common Name	Scientific Name
Calabazilla	*Cucurbita foetidissima*
Manroot, Wild-Cucumber	*Marah macrocarpus*

ERICACEAE - HEATH FAMILY

Common Name	Scientific Name
Del Mar Manzanita	*Arctostaphylos glandulosa* ssp. *crassifolia*
Mission Manzanita	*Xylococcus bicolor*

EUPHORBIACEAE - SPURGE FAMILY

Common Name	Scientific Name
Small-seed Sandmat	*Chamaesyce polycarpa* var. *polycarpa*
	Croton californicus var. *tenuis*
Doveweed	*Eremocarpus setigerus*
Cliff Spurge	*Euphorbia misera*
* Petty Spurge	*Euphorbia peplus*
Reticulate-seed Spurge	*Euphorbia spathulata*
* Castor-Bean	*Ricinus communis*

FABACEAE - PEA FAMILY

Common Name	Scientific Name
* Golden Wattle	*Acacia longifolia*
False-Indigo	*Amorpha fruticosa* var. *occidentalis*
White Dwarf Locoweed	*Astragalus didymocarpus* var. *didymocarpus*
Locoweed	*Astragalus trichopodus* ssp. *leucopsis*
Coastal Deerweed	*Lotus scoparius* ssp. *scoparius*
Bishop's Lotus	*Lotus strigosus* var. *strigosus*
Lupine	*Lupinus bicolor* ssp. *microphyllus*
Lupine	*Lupinus densiflorus* ssp. *austrocollium*
Stinging Lupine	*Lupinus hirsutissimus*
Bluebonnet	*Lupinus succulentus*
Collar Lupine	*Lupinus truncatus*
* California Bur-Clover	*Medicago polymorpha*
* White Sweet Clover	*Melilotus albus*
* Indian Sweet Clover	*Melilotus indicus*

FAGACEAE - OAK FAMILY

Common Name	Scientific Name
Scrub Oak	*Quercus dumosa*

FRANKENIACEAE - FRANKENIA FAMILY

Common Name	Scientific Name
Alkali-Heath	*Frankenia salina*

GENTIANACEAE - GENTIAN FAMILY

Common Name	Scientific Name
Canchalagua	*Centaurium venustum*

GERANIACEAE - GERANIUM FAMILY
   * Long-beak Filaree — *Erodium botrys*
   * Red-stem Filaree — *Erodium cicutarium*
   * White-stem Filaree — *Erodium moschatum*
   Carolina Geranium — *Geranium carolinianum*
GROSSULARIACEAE - CURRANT FAMILY
   Winter Currant — *Ribes indecorum*
   Fuchsia-flowered Gooseberry — *Ribes speciosum*
HYDROPHYLLACEAE - WATERLEAF FAMILY
   Yerba Santa — *Eriodictyon crassifolium*
   Eucrypta chrysanthemifolia var. *chrysanthemifolia*
   Nemophila menziesii
   Caterpillar Phacelia — *Phacelia cicutaria* ssp. *hispida*
   Wild-Heliotrope — *Phacelia distans*
   Phacelia parryi
   Fiesta-Flower — *Pholistoma auritum*
   Pholistoma racemosum
LAMIACEAE - MINT FAMILY
   * Horehound — *Marrubium vulgare*
   White Sage — *Salvia apiana*
   Cleveland Sage — *Salvia clevelandii*
   Chia — *Salvia columbariae*
   Black Sage — *Salvia mellifera*
   Stachys rigida ssp. *quercetorum*
LENNOACEAE - SANDFOOD FAMILY
   Sand Plant — *Pholisma arenarium*
MALVACEAE - MALLOW FAMILY
   Mesa Bushmallow — *Malacothamnus fasciculatus*
   * Cheeseweed — *Malva parviflora*
   Alkali Mallow — *Malvella leprosa*
MYOPORACEAE - MYOPORUM FAMILY
   * Ngaio — *Myoporum laetum*
NYCTAGINACEAE - FOUR-O'CLOCK FAMILY
   Red Sand-Verbena — *Abronia maritima*
   Beach Sand-Verbena — *Abronia umbellata*
   Wishbone Plant — *Mirabilis californica*
ONAGRACEAE - EVENING-PRIMROSE FAMILY
   Southern Sun-cup — *Camissonia bistorta*
   Beach Evening-Primrose — *Camissonia cheiranthifolia* ssp. *suffruticosa*
   Camissonia micrantha
   Clarkia purpurea ssp. *quadrivulnera*
   California-Fuchsia — *Epilobium canum* ssp. *angustifolium*
   Great Marsh Evening-Primrose — *Oenothera elata* ssp. *hirsutissima*
OROBANCHACEAE - BROOM-RAPE FAMILY
   Beach Broom-Rate — *Orobanche parishii* ssp. *brachyloba*
OXALIDACEAE - WOOD-SORREL FAMILY
   California Oxalis — *Oxalis albicans* ssp. *californica*
   * Bermuda-Buttercup — *Oxalis cernua*
PAEONIACEAE - PEONY FAMILY
   California Peony — *Paeonia californica*

PAPAVERACEAE - POPPY FAMILY
    California Bush (Tree) Poppy — *Dendromecon rigida* ssp. *rigida*
    * Coastal California Poppy — *Eschscholzia californica* var. *californica*
    Cream Cups — *Platystemon californicus* var. *californicus*
    Wind Poppy — *Stylomecon heterophylla*
PLANTAGINACEAE - PLANTAIN FAMILY
    Dot-seed Plantain — *Plantago erecta* ssp. *erecta*
PLUMBAGINACEAE - LEADWORT FAMILY
    San Diego Rosemary (Sea Lavender) — *Limonium californicum* var. *mexicanum*
    * Perez Rosemary — *Limonium perezii*
POLEMONIACEAE - PHLOX FAMILY
    Ground Pink — *Linanthus dianthiflorus*
    Skunkweed — *Navarretia hamata*
POLYGONACEAE - BUCKWHEAT FAMILY
    California Spine-Flower — *Chorizanthe californica*
    Lastarriaea — *Chorizanthe coriacea*
    Prostrate Spine-Flower — *Chorizanthe procumbens* var. *procumbens*
    Turkish Rugging — *Chorizanthe staticoides* ssp. *staticoides*
    Flat-top (California) Buckwheat — *Eriogonum fasciculatum* ssp. *fasciculatum*
    Bluff Buckwheat — *Eriogonum parvifolium*
    Dune-Thread — *Nemocaulis denudata* var. *denudata*
    * Knotweed — *Polygonum arenastrum*
    Granny's Hairnet — *Pterostegia drymarioides*
    * Curly Dock — *Rumex crispus*
    Willow-leaf Dock — *Rumex salicifolius* var. *salicifolius*
PORTULACACEAE - PURSLANE FAMILY
    Red Maids — *Calandrinia ciliata* var. *menziesii*
    Sea Kisses — *Calandrinia maritima*
    Common Calyptridium — *Calyptridium monandrum*
    Common Miner's-Lettuce — *Claytonia perfoliata*
    Narrow-leaf Miner's Lettuce — *Claytonia perfoliata* var. *parviflora*
PRIMULACEAE - PRIMROSE FAMILY
    * Scarlet Pimpernel — *Anagallis arvensis*
    Padre's Shooting Star — *Dodecatheon clevelandii* ssp. *clevelandii*
RANUNCULACEAE - CROWFOOT FAMILY
    Pipestem Virgin's-Bower — *Clematis lasiantha*
    Virgin's Bower — *Clematis pauciflora*
    Scarlet Larkspur — *Delphinium cardinale*
    Maritime Larkspur — *Delphinium parryi* var. *maritimum*
    Mouse-Tail — *Myosurus minimus* var. *apus*
RESEDACEAE - MIGNONETTE FAMILY
    Narrowleaf Oligomeris — *Oligomeris linifolia*
RHAMNACEAE - BUCKTHORN FAMILY
    Ramona-Lilac — *Ceanothus tomentosus* ssp. *olivaceus*
    Coast White-lilac — *Ceanothus verrucosus*
      (Warty-stemmed Ceanothus)
    Spiny Redberry — *Rhamnus crocea*

ROSACEAE - ROSE FAMILY
- Common Chamise — *Adenostoma fasciculatum*
- Western Lady's-Mantle — *Alchemilla occidentalis*
- Coastal Mountain-Mahogany — *Cercocarpus minutiflorus*
- Toyon (Christmas Berry) — *Heteromeles salicifolia*
- Cinquefoil — *Potentilla glandulosa*

RUBIACEAE - MADDER FAMILY
- Narrow-leaf Bedstraw — *Galium angustifolium*
- * Common Bedstraw — *Galium aparine*
- Nuttall's Bedstraw — *Galium nuttallii* ssp. *nuttallii*
- Laura May's Bedstraw — *Galium porrigens* var. *porrigens*

RUTACEAE - RUE FAMILY
- Coast Spice Bush (Bushrue) — *Cneoridium dumosum*

SALICACEAE - WILLOW FAMILY
- Black Willow — *Salix gooddingii* var. *variabilis*
- Arroyo Willow — *Salix lasiolepis* var. *lasiolepis*

SAURURACEAE - LIZARD-TAIL FAMILY
- Yerba Mansa — *Anemopsis californica*

SAXIFRAGACEAE - SAXIFRAGE FAMILY
- Coast Jepsonia — *Jepsonia parryi*
- Woodland Star — *Lithophragma affine* ssp. *affine*

SCROPHULARIACEAE - FIGWORT FAMILY
- Snapdragon — *Antirrhinum coulterianum*
- Climbing Snapdragon — *Antirrhinum kelloggii*
- Nuttall's Snapdragon — *Antirrhinum nuttallianum*
- Coast Paint-Brush — *Castilleja affinis* ssp. *affinis*
- Felt Paint-Brush — *Castilleja foliolosa*
- Chinese Houses — *Collinsia heterophylla*
- Dark-tip Bird's Beak — *Cordylanthus rigida*
- Coast Bush (Red) Monkeyflower — *Diplacus puniceus*
- Large Blue Toadflax — *Linaria canadensis* var. *texana*
- Slope Semiphore — *Mimulus brevipes*
- Red Owl's-Clover — *Orthocarpus purpurascens* var. *purpurascens*
- California Bee Plant — *Scrophularia californica* var. *floribunda*

SOLANACEAE - NIGHTSHADE FAMILY
- Western Jimsonweed — *Datura wrightii*
- * Common Desert Thorn — *Lycium brevipes* var. *brevipes*
- California Desert Thorn — *Lycium californicum*
- Wallace's Tobacco — *Nicotiana bigelovii* var. *wallacei*
- * Tree Tobacco — *Nicotiana glauca*
- White Nightshade — *Solanum americanum*
- Douglas' Nightshade — *Solanum douglasii*
- Parish's Nightshade — *Solanum parishii*
- Chaparral Nightshade — *Solanum xanti* var. *intermedium*

TAMARICACEAE - TAMARISK FAMILY
- * Tamarisk — *Tamarix parviflora*
- * Salt-Cedar — *Tamarix ramosissima*

URTICACEAE - NETTLE FAMILY
- Western Nettle — *Hesperocnide tenella*
- Western Pellitory — *Parietaria hespera* var. *californica*
- * Common Nettle — *Urtica urens*

PLANTS (CONTINUED)	* = Non-native Taxa
Common Name	**Scientific Name**

VIOLACEAE - VIOLET FAMILY
   Yellow Johnny Jump-Ups — *Viola pedunculata*

ZYGOPHYLLACEAE - CALTROP FAMILY
   * Puncture Vine — *Tribulus terrestris*

FLOWERING PLANTS - MONOCOTYLEDONS

AGAVACEAE - AGAVE FAMILY
   Coastal Agave — *Agave shawii*
   Mojave Yucca — *Yucca schidigera*
   Our Lord's Candle — *Yucca whipplei*

ALLIACEAE - ONION FAMILY
   Red-skin Onion — *Allium haematochiton*
   Common Golden-Stars — *Bloomeria crocea* ssp. *crocea*
   Wild-Hyacinth — *Dichelostemma pulchellum*
   Cleveland's Golden-Stars — *Muilla clevelandii*

CYPERACEAE - SEDGE FAMILY
   Chaparral Sedge — *Carex triquetra*
   Tall Flatsedge — *Cyperus eragrostis*
   California Bulrush — *Scirpus californicus*
   Prairie Bulrush — *Scirpus robustus*

IRIDACEAE - IRIS FAMILY
   Blue-eyed-Grass — *Sisyrinchium bellum*

JUNCACEAE - RUSH FAMILY
   Southwestern Spiny Rush — *Juncus acutus* ssp. *leopoldii*
   Mexican Rush — *Juncus mexicanus*

LILIACEAE - LILY FAMILY
   * Hollow-Stem Asphodel — *Asphodelus fistulosus*
   Splendid Mariposa-Lily — *Calochortus splendens*
   Weed's Mariposa-Lily — *Calochortus weedii* var. *weedii*
   Small-Flower Soap-Plant — *Chlorogalum parviflorum*
   Fremont's Camas — *Zigadenus fremontii* var. *fremontii*

ORCHIDACEAE - ORCHID FAMILY
   Slender-spire Piperia — *Habenaria unalascensis*

POACEAE - GRASS FAMILY
   * Giant Cane — *Arundo donax*
   * Slender Oat — *Avena barbata*
   * Wild Oat — *Avena fatua*
   California Brome — *Bromus carinatus*
   * Ripgut Grass — *Bromus diandrus*
   * Soft Chess — *Bromus mollis*
   * Red Brome — *Bromus rubens*
   * Pampas Grass — *Cortaderia jubata*
   * Bermuda Grass — *Cynodon dactylon*
   Coastal Salt Grass — *Distichlis spicata*
   Giant Rye — *Elymus condensatus*
   * Reed Fescue — *Festuca arundinacea*
   * Glaucous Barley — *Hordeum murinum* ssp. *glaucum*
   * Hare Barley — *Hordeum murinum* ssp. *leporinum*
   Junegrass — *Koeleria macrantha*
   * Goldentop — *Lamarckia aurea*
   * English Ryegrass — *Lolium perenne*
   Coast Range Melic — *Melica imperfecta*

PLANTS (CONTINUED)	* = Non-native Taxa
Common Name	Scientific Name

POACEAE - GRASS FAMILY (continued)

Common Name	Scientific Name
Salt-cedar	*Monanthochloe littoralis*
Little-seed Muhly	*Muhlenbergia microsperma*
European Sicklegrass	*Parapholis incurva*
* African Fountain-grass	*Pennisetum setaceum*
Canary Grass	*Phalaris caroliniana*
* Annual Beardgrass	*Polypogon monspeliensis*
* Natal Grass	*Rhynchelytrum roseum*
* Mediterranean Schismus	*Schismus barbatus*
Giant Stipa	*Stipa coronata*
Foothill Needlegrass	*Stipa lepida*
Purple Needlegrass	*Stipa pulchra*
	Vulpia megalura
* Foxtail Fescue	*Vulpia myuros*
Tufted Fescue	*Vulpia octoflora* var. *hirtella*

POTAMOGETONACEAE - PONDWEED FAMILY

Common Name	Scientific Name
Beakfruit Sea-Tassle	*Ruppia maritima*

TYPHACEAE - CAT-TAIL FAMILY

Common Name	Scientific Name
Cat-tail	*Typha domingensis*
Soft Flag Cat-tail	*Typha latifolia*

ZOSTERACEAE - EELGRASS FAMILY

Common Name	Scientific Name
Torrey's Surf-Grass	*Phyllospadix torreyi*
Common Eelgrass	*Zostera marina*

INVERTEBRATE ANIMALS	L = Lagoon O = Ocean/Beach M = Marsh U = Upland

Common Name	Scientific Name	Habitat

MOLLUSKS

BIVALVES

Common Name	Scientific Name	Habitat
Little Egg Cockle	*Laevicardium substriatum*	L
Bean Clam	*Donax gouldii*	O
Bent-nosed Clam	*Macoma nasuta*	L
California Mussel	*Mytilus californianus*	O
Bay Mussel	*Mytilus edulis*	L
Little-neck Clam	*Protothaca staminea*	O,L
Speckled Scallop	*Argopecten circularis/aequisulcatus*	L
Broad-eared Scallop	*Pecten latiauratus*	O,L
Gaper Clam	*Tresus nuttallii*	O,L
Jackknife Clam	*Tagelus californianus*	O,L
Pismo Clam	*Tivela stultorum*	O
Rough Piddock	*Zirfaea pilsbryi*	O,L

UNIVALVES

Common Name	Scientific Name	Habitat
Wavy Topshell	*Astraea undosa*	O
Bubble Shell	*Bulla gouldiana*	L
Black Abalone	*Haliotis cracherodii*	O
Green Abalone	*Haliotis fulgens*	O
Red Abalone	*Haliotis rufescens*	O
Salt-marsh Snail	*Melampus olivaceus*	M
Sea Slug	*Navanax inermis*	L
Purple Olive	*Olivella biplicata*	O,L

96

INVERTEBRATE ANIMALS (CONTINUED)	L = Lagoon O = Ocean/Beach M = Marsh U = Upland	
Common Name	**Scientific Name**	**Habitat**

ECHINODERMS		
Common Sand Dollar	*Dendraster excentricus*	O,L
Giant Red Sea Urchin	*Strongylocentrotus franciscanus*	O
Purple Sea Urchin	*Strongylocentrotus purpuratus*	O
CRUSTACEANS		
Limpets	*Acmaea* spp.	O
Ghost Shrimp	*Callianassa californiensis*	L
Crayfish	*Cambarus clarkii*	M
Sand Crab	*Emerita analoga*	O
Mud (Mud-flat) Crab	*Hemigrapsus oregonensis*	L,M
Rock Louse	*Liggia occidentalis*	O
Striped Shore Crab	*Pachygrapsus crassipes*	O,L,M
Spiny Lobster	*Panulirus interruptus*	O
Fiddler Crab	*Uca crenulata*	L
INSECTS[1]		
DERMAPTERA - EARWIGS		
Ring-legged Earwig	*Euborellia annulipes*	U
ORTHOPTERA - GRASSHOPPERS AND ALLIES		
Clear-winged Grasshopper	*Camnula pellucida*	U
Field Cricket	*Gryllus* sp.	U
Praying Mantis	Mantidae	U
Short-horned Grasshopper	*Melanoplus* sp.	U
Tree Cricket	*Oecanthus* sp.	U
Jerusalem Cricket	*Stenopelmatus* sp.	U
Long-horned Grasshopper	Tettigoniidae	U
ISOPTERA - TERMITES		
Western Subterranean Termite	*Reticulitermes kesperus*	U
EMBIOPTERA - WEBSPINNERS		
Webspinner	*Haploembia solieri*	U
ODONATA - DAMSELFLIES AND DRAGONFLIES		
Blue Darner Dragonfly	*Aeshna* sp.	M
Damselfly	*Enallagma* sp.	M
Skimmer Dragonfly	*Libellula* sp.	M
NEUROPTERA - LACEWINGS		
Green Lacewing	*Chrysopa* sp.	U
Antlions	Myrmeleontidae	U
THYSANOPTERA - THRIPS		
Western Flower Thrips	*Frankliniella occidentalis*	U
HOMOPTERA - HOPPERS		
Cicada	*Cicada* spp.	U
Leafhopper	*Homalodisca lacerta*	U
HEMIPTERA - TRUE BUGS		
	Chlorochroa sp.	U
Seed Bug	*Lygaeus reclivatus*	U
Harlequin Bug	*Murgentia histrionica*	U

---

[1] Many of the insects and spiders no doubt occur also in transition zones and in the marsh. Many other insect species also occur in the Reserve.

Common Name	Scientific Name	Habitat
HEMIPTERA - TRUE BUGS (continued)		
Plant Bug	*Lygus* sp.	U
Assassin Bug	*Zelus* sp.	U
COLEOPTERA - BEETLES		
Predaceous Ground Beetle	*Brachinus* sp.	U
Weevil	*Brachyrhinus* sp.	U
Tiger Beetle	*Cicindela hirticollis*	U
Western Spotted Cucumber Beetle	*Diabrotica undecimpunctata*	U
Ground Beetle	*Eleodes* sp.	U
Convergent Lady Beetle	*Hippodamia convergens*	U
June Beetle	*Perocotalpa ursina*	U
Bark Beetle	*Pityophthorus carmeli*	U
Five-spined Engraver Beetle	*Ips paraconfusus*	U
Rain Beetle	*Pleocoma puncticollis*	U
Lady-bug Beetle	*Scymnus ornatus*	U
Rove Beetle	*Thinopinus* sp.	U
DIPTERA - FLIES		
Mosquitos	*Aedes, Anopheles* and *Culex* spp.	L,M,U
Robber Flies	Asilidae	U
Midges	Chironomidae	M,U
Deer Fly	*Chrysops* sp.	U
Seaweed Fly	*Coelopa vanduzeei*	O,L
Kelp Flies	*Fucellia costalis/F. rufitibia*	O,L
Flower Flies	Syrphidae	U
Crane Flies	Tipulidae	U
LEPIDOPTERA - BUTTERFLIES		
Gulf Fritillary	*Agraulis vanillae*	U
Sara Orange-Tip	*Anthocharis sara*	U
Mormon Metal-mark	*Apodemia mormo*	U
Pigmy Blue	*Brephidium exilis*	U
Large Sulphur	*Catopsilia eubule sennae*	U
Ringlet Butterfly	*Coenonympha tullia*	U
Boisduval's Sulphur	*Colias eurytheme*	U
Queen Butterfly	*Danaus berenice*	U
Monarch Butterfly	*Danaus plexippus*	U
Brown Skipper	*Srynnis propertius*	U
Checkerspot	*Euphydryas editha*	U
Nicippe Yellow	*Eurema nicippe*	U
California Sister	*Adelpha bredowii californica*	U
Dwarf Sulphur	*Nathalis iole*	U
Mourning Cloak	*Nymphalis antiopa*	U
Blue	*Philotes battoides*	U
Checkered White	*Pieris protodice*	U
Cabbage Butterfly	*Pieris rapae*	U
Western Tiger Swallowtail	*Papilio rutulus*	U
Anise Swallowtail	*Papilio zelicaon*	U
Buckeye	*Precis lavinia*	U
Red Admiral	*Vanessa atalanta*	U
Painted Lady	*Vanessa cardui*	U
West Coast Lady	*Vanessa carye*	U

INVERTEBRATE ANIMALS (CONTINUED)	L = Lagoon O = Ocean/Beach M = Marsh U = Upland	
Common Name	**Scientific Name**	**Habitat**

HYMENOPTERA - BEES AND WASPS

Common Name	Scientific Name	Habitat
Honey Bee	*Apis mellifera*	U
Bumble Bee	*Bombus* sp.	U
Tarantula Hawk	*Pepsis chrysothemis*	U
Harvester Ant	*Pogonomyrmex* sp.	U
Paper Wasp	*Polistes* sp.	U
Thread-waisted Wasp	*Sphex vulgaris*	U

SPIDERS

Common Name	Scientific Name	Habitat
Funnel Web Weavers	Agelenidae	U
Orb Weavers	*Argiope argentata/A. aurantia*	U
Trapdoor Spider	*Bothryocyrtum californicum*	U
Sac Spiders	Clubionidae	U
Black Widow	*Latrodectus* sp.	U
Wolf Spiders	Lycosidae	U
Lynx Spiders	Oxyopidae	U
Jumping Spiders	Thomisidae	U
Zodariids	Zodariidae	U

VERTEBRATE ANIMALS	L = Lagoon O = Ocean/Beach M = Marsh U = Upland	
Common Name	**Scientific Name**	**Habitat**

FISHES

SHARKS

Common Name	Scientific Name	Habitat
Gray Smoothhound	*Mustelus californicus*	O
Leopard Shark	*Triakis semifasciata*	O,L

RAYS

Common Name	Scientific Name	Habitat
Bat Ray	*Myliobatis californica*	O
Shovelnose Guitarfish	*Rhinobatos productus*	O
Round Sting Ray	*Urolophus halleri*	O,L

KILLIFISHES

Common Name	Scientific Name	Habitat
California Killifish	*Fundulus parvipinnis*	L
Western Mosquitofish	*Gambusia affinis*	L,M

PIPEFISHES

Common Name	Scientific Name	Habitat
Bay Pipefish	*Syngnathus leptorhynchus*	L
Barred Pipefish	*Syngnathus auliscus*	L

SILVERSIDES

Common Name	Scientific Name	Habitat
Bay Topsmelt	*Atherinops affinis littoralis*	O,L
Grunion	*Leuresthes tenuis*	O

FLATFISHES

Common Name	Scientific Name	Habitat
Diamond Turbot	*Hypsopsetta guttulata*	O,L
California Halibut	*Paralichthys californicus*	O,L

MULLETS

Common Name	Scientific Name	Habitat
Striped Mullet	*Mugil cephalus*	L

ANCHOVIES

Common Name	Scientific Name	Habitat
Deep Bodied Anchovy	*Anchoa compressa*	L

SEA BASSES

Common Name	Scientific Name	Habitat
Spotted Sand Bass	*Paralabrax maculatofasciatus*	L

Common Name	Scientific Name	Habitat
NIBBLERS		
Opaleye	*Girella nigricans*	O,L
VIVIPAROUS PERCHES		
Barred Surfperch	*Amphistichus argenteus*	O
Black Seaperch	*Embiotoca jacksoni*	O
Walleye Surfperch	*Hyperprosopon argenteum*	O
CROAKERS		
California Corbina	*Menticirrhus undulatus*	O
Spotfin Croaker	*Roncador stearnsii*	O
Yellowfin Croaker	*Umbrina roncador*	O
SCULPINS		
Southern Staghorn Sculpin	*Leptocottus armatus australis*	O,L
GOBIES		
Yellowfin Goby	*Acanthogobius flavimanus*	L
Arrow Goby	*Clevelandia ios*	L
Mudsucker	*Gillichthys mirabilis*	L
AMPHIBIANS		
PLETHODONTIDAE - LUNGLESS SALAMANDERS		
Garden Slender Salamander	*Batrachoseps major*	M,U
Arboreal Salamander	*Aneides lugubris*	M,U
HYLIDAE - TREEFROGS AND RELATIVES		
Pacific Chorus Frog	*Pseudacris regilla*	M
BUFONIDAE - TRUE TOADS		
Western Toad	*Bufo boreas*	M
RANIDAE - TRUE FROGS		
Red-legged Frog	*Rana aurora*	L,M
Bullfrog	*Rana catesbeiana*	L,M
PELOBATIDAE - SPADEFOOT TOADS		
Western Spadefoot	*Spea hammondi*	M,U
REPTILES		
CHELONIIDAE - SEA TURTLES		
Green Turtle	*Chelonia mydas*	O
Pacific Loggerhead	*Caretta caretta gigas*	O
Pacific Ridley	*Lepidochelys olivacea*	O
DERMOCHELYIDAE - LEATHERBACK TURTLES		
Leatherback	*Dermochelys coriacea*	O
PHRYNOSOMATIDAE		
Western Fence Lizard	*Sceloporus occidentalis*	U
Side-blotched Lizard	*Uta stansburiana*	O,U
Coast Horned Lizard	*Phrynosoma coronatum*	U
SCINCIDAE - SKINKS		
Western Skink	*Eumeces skiltonianus*	O,U
TEIIDAE - WHIPTAILS AND RELATIVES		
Orangethroat Whiptail	*Cnemidophorus hyperythrus*	U
Western Whiptail	*Cnemidophorus tigris*	U
ANGUIDAE - ALLIGATOR LIZARDS AND RELATIVES		
California Legless Lizard	*Anniella nigra*	O,U
Southern Alligator Lizard	*Elgaria multicarinatus*	M,U

Common Name	Scientific Name	Habitat
LEPTOTYPHLOPIDAE - SLENDER BLIND SNAKES		
Western Blind Snake	*Leptotyphlops humilis*	U
BOIDAE - BOAS		
Rosy Boa	*Lichanura trivirgata*	U
COLUBRIDAE - COLUBRID SNAKES		
Ringneck Snake	*Diadophis punctatus*	U
Racer	*Coluber constrictor*	U
Coachwhip	*Masticophis flagellum*	U
California Striped Racer	*Masticophis lateralis*	U
Western Patch-nosed Snake	*Salvadora hexalepis*	U
Glossy Snake	*Arizona elegans*	O,U
Gopher Snake	*Pituophis catenifer*	O,U
Common Kingsnake	*Lampropeltis getulus*	O,U
Long-nosed Snake	*Rhinocheilus lecontei*	U
Two-striped Garter Snake	*Thamnophis hammondi*	M
Western Black-headed Snake	*Tantilla planiceps*	M
Night Snake	*Hypsiglena torquata*	U
VIPERIDAE - VIPERS		
Red Diamond Rattlesnake	*Crotalus ruber*	U
Southern Pacific Rattlesnake	*Crotalus viridis helleri*	U
MAMMALS		
DIDELPHIDAE - OPOSSUMS		
Virginia Opossum	*Didelphis virginiana*	U
SORICIDAE - SHREWS		
Ornate Shrew	*Sorex ornatus*	M,U
Desert Shrew	*Notiosorex crawfordi*	M,U
TALPIDAE - MOLES		
Broad-footed Mole	*Scapanus latimanus*	U
VESPERTILIONIDAE - VESPERTILIONID BATS		
Red Bat	*Lasiurus borealis*	M,U
Hoary Bat	*Lasiurus cinereus*	M,U
LEPORIDAE - RABBITS AND HARES		
Brush Rabbit	*Sylvilagus bachmani*	U
Desert Cottontail	*Sylvilagus audubonii*	M,U
Black-tailed Jackrabbit	*Lepus californicus*	M,U
SCIURIDAE - SQUIRRELS, CHIPMUNKS, AND MARMOTS		
California (Beechey) Ground Squirrel	*Spermophilus beecheyi*	O,M,U
GEOMYIDAE - POCKET GOPHERS		
Botta's Pocket Gopher	*Thomomys bottae*	U
HETEROMYIDAE - POCKET MICE AND KANGAROO RATS		
San Diego Pocket Mouse	*Perognathus fallax*	M,U
California Pocket Mouse	*Perognathus californicus*	M,U
Pacific Kangaroo Rat	*Dipodomys agilis*	M,U
MURIDAE - RATS, MICE, AND VOLES		
Western Harvest Mouse	*Reithrodontomys megalotis*	M,U
Cactus Mouse	*Peromyscus eremicus*	U
Deer Mouse	*Peromyscus maniculatus*	M,U
Southern Grasshopper Mouse	*Onychomys torridus*	M,U
Desert/Dusky-footed Woodrat	*Neotoma lepida/N. fuscipes*	U
California Vole	*Microtus californicus*	M,U

Common Name	Scientific Name	Habitat
MURIDAE - RATS, MICE, AND VOLES (continued)		
Black Rat	*Rattus rattus*	M.U
House Mouse	*Mus musculus*	M,U
CANIDAE - FOXES, WOLVES, AND RELATIVES		
Coyote	*Canis latrans*	U
Gray Fox	*Urocyon cinereoargenteus*	U
PROCYONIDAE - RACCOONS AND RELATIVES		
Raccoon	*Procyon lotor*	M,U
MUSTELIDAE - WEASELS, BADGERS, AND RELATIVES		
Long-tailed Weasel	*Mustela frenata*	U
Badger	*Taxidea taxus*	U
Western Spotted Skunk	*Spilogale gracilis*	U
Striped Skunk	*Mephitis mephitis*	U
FELIDAE - CATS		
Bobcat	*Lynx rufus*	U
OTARIIDAE - EARED SEALS		
California Sea Lion	*Zalophus californianus*	O
PHOCIDAE - HAIR SEALS		
Harbor Seal	*Phoca vitulina*	O
CERVIDAE - DEER, ELK, AND RELATIVES		
Mule Deer	*Odocoileus hemionus*	U
ZIPHIIDAE - BEAKED WHALES		
Archbeak Whale	*Mesoplodon carlhubbsi*	O
Goosebeak Whale	*Ziphius cavirostris*	O
PHYSETERIDAE - SPERM WHALES		
Sperm Whale	*Physeter catodon*	O
KOGIIDAE - PYGMY SPERM WHALES		
Pygmy Sperm Whale	*Kogia breviceps*	O
DELPHINIDAE - DOLPHINS AND PORPOISES		
Striped Dolphin	*Stenella caeruleoalba*	O
Common Dolphin	*Delphinus delphis*	O
Pacific Bottlenose Dolphin	*Tursiops gilli*	O
Pacific White-sided Dolphin	*Lagenorhynchus obliquidens*	O
Killer Whale	*Orcinus orca*	O
Pilot Whale/Common Blackfish	*Globicephala melaena*	O
Dall Porpoise	*Phocoenoides dalli*	O
ESCHRICHTIIDAE- GRAY WHALES		
Gray Whale	*Eschrichtius gibbosus*	O

Seasonal Abundance Code	Habitat Code	Status Code
5 = Abundant 4 = Common 3 = Fairly Common 2 = Occasional 1 = Rare	O = Ocean B = Beach L = Lagoon W = Riparian Willow C = Chaparral P = Torrey Pines	* = Current Breeder ? = Possible Breeder + = Former Breeder # = Endangered

VERTEBRATE ANIMALS (CONTINUED)

Common Name	Scientific Name	F	W	S	Su	Habitats	Status
BIRDS							
GAVIIDAE - LOON							
Red-throated Loon	*Gavia stellata*	2	3	2		O	
Pacific Loon	*Gavia pacifica*	2	3	2		O	
Common Loon	*Gavia immer*	2	3	2		O	
PODICIPEDIDAE - GREBES							
Pied-billed Grebe	*Podilymbus podiceps*	4	4	4	4	L	*
Horned Grebe	*Podiceps auritus*	2	2	2		L	
Eared Grebe	*Podiceps nigricollis*	3	3	3	1	L	?
Western Grebe	*Aechmophorus occidentalis*	4	5	5	1	OL	
Clark's Grebe	*Aechmophorus clarki*	2	2	2		OL	
PROCELLARIIDAE - SHEARWATERS, FULMARS							
Pink-footed Shearwater	*Puffinus creatopus*	1	1			O	
Sooty Shearwater	*Puffinus griseus*	1	1	1		O	
Black-vented Shearwater	*Puffinus opisthomelas*	2	3	2		O	
PELECANIDAE - PELICANS							
American White Pelican	*Pelecanus erythrorhynchos*	1		1		L	
Brown Pelican	*Pelecanus occidentalis*	4	4	3	4	OL	#
PHALACROCORACIDAE - CORMORANTS							
Double-crested Cormorant	*Phalacrocorax auritus*	4	4	4	3	OL	
Brandt's Cormorant	*Phalacrocorax penicillatus*	2	2	2	2	O	
Pelagic Cormorant	*Phalacrocorax pelagicus*	1	1	1	1	O	
ARDEIDAE - HERONS AND BITTERS							
American Bittern	*Botaurus lentiginosus*		1			L	
Great Blue Heron	*Ardea herodias*	4	4	3	4	L	*
Great Egret	*Casmerodius alba*	4	4	3	3	L	
Snowy Egret	*Egretta thula*	4	3	3	3	L	
Tricolored Heron	*Egretta tricolor*	1	1	1		L	
Cattle Egret	*Bubulcus ibis*	1	1			L	
Green-backed Heron	*Butorides striatus*	2	2	2	2	L	*
Black-crowned Night-Heron	*Nycticorax nycticorax*	3	2	2	4	L	
THRESKIORNITHIDAE - IBISES AND SPOONBILLS							
White-faced Ibis	*Plegadis chihi*	2	2	2	1	L	
ANATIDAE - SWANS, GEESE, AND DUCKS							
Brant	*Branta bernicla*			2		L	
Canada Goose	*Branta canadensis*		1			L	
Green-winged Teal	*Anas crecca*	3	3	3		L	
Mallard	*Anas platyrhynchos*	4	4	5	5	L	*
Northern Pintail	*Anas acuta*	3	4	3		L	

Common Name	Scientific Name	Seasonal Abundance				Habitats	Status
		F	W	S	Su		
ANATIDAE - SWANS, GEESE, AND DUCKS (continued)							
Blue-winged Teal	*Anas discors*	2	2	2		L	
Cinnamon Teal	*Anas cyanoptera*	3	3	4	2	L	
Northern Shoveler	*Anas clypeata*	3	4	3		L	
Gadwall	*Anas strepera*	3	3	4	4	L	?
Eurasian Wigeon	*Anas penelope*	1				L	
American Wigeon	*Anas americana*	5	4	4	1	L	
Canvasback	*Aythya valisineria*		1			L	
Redhead	*Aythya americana*	2	2	2		L	+
Lesser Scaup	*Aythya affinis*	3	4	4		L	
Black Scoter	*Melanitta nigra*		1			O	
Surf Scoter	*Melanitta perspicillata*	4	5	4	1	O	
White-winged Scoter	*Melanitta fusca*	1	1	1		O	
Bufflehead	*Bucephala albeola*	2	4	3		L	
Red-breasted Merganser	*Mergus serrator*		2	2		L	
Ruddy Duck	*Oxyura jamaicensis*	3	4	4	2	L	?
CATHARTIDAE - AMERICAN VULTURES							
Turkey Vulture	*Cathartes aura*	1	1	1		CP	
ACCIPITRIDAE - HAWKS AND HARRIERS							
Osprey	*Pandion haliaetus*	2	2	2		L	
Black-shouldered Kite	*Elanus caeruleus*	3	3	2	3	L	?
Northern Harrier	*Circus cyaneus*	2	2	1		LW	+
Sharp-shinned Hawk	*Accipiter striatus*	2	2	1		WCP	
Cooper's Hawk	*Accipiter cooperii*	2	2	2		WCP	*
Red-shouldered Hawk	*Buteo lineatus*	2	2	2	2	WCP	*
Red-tailed Hawk	*Buteo jamaicensis*	3	3	3	2	CP	*
Golden Eagle	*Aquila chrysaetos*	1	1	1	1		
FALCONIDAE - CARACARAS AND FALCONS							
American Kestrel	*Falco sparverius*	3	3	3	3	CP	*
Merlin	*Falco columbarius*		1			L	
Peregrine Falcon	*Falco peregrinus*	1	1			L	#
Prairie Falcon	*Falco mexicanus*		1			L	
PHASIANIDAE - QUAILS, PHEASANTS, AND RELATIVES							
California Quail	*Callipepla californica*	3	3	3	3	C	*
RALLIDAE - RAILS, GALLINULES, AND COOTS							
Virginia Rail	*Rallus limicola*	2	2	2	1	L	?
RALLIDAE - RAILS, GALLINULES, AND COOTS (continued)							
Sora	*Porzana carolina*	2	2	2		L	
American Coot	*Fulica americana*	5	5	5	3	L	?
CHARADRIIDAE - PLOVERS AND RELATIVES							
Black-bellied Plover	*Pluvialis squatarola*	3	2	2	2	L	
Lesser Golden-Plover	*Pluvialis dominica*		1			L	
Snowy Plover	*Charadrius alexandrinus*	3	3	3	2	BL	*#
Semipalmated Plover	*Charadrius semipalmatus*	3	2	2		L	
Killdeer	*Charadrius vociferus*	3	3	3	3	L	*
RECURVIROSTRIDAE - AVOCETS AND STILTS							
Black-necked Stilt	*Himantopus mexicanus*	3	2	3	3	L	*
American Avocet	*Recurvirostra americana*	1	2	2		L	

Common Name	Scientific Name	Seasonal Abundance				Habitats	Status
		F	W	S	Su		
SCOLOPACIDAE - SANDPIPERS AND RELATIVES							
Greater Yellowlegs	*Tringa melanoleuca*	3	2	2	2	L	
Lesser Yellowlegs	*Tringa flavipes*	2	2	1	1	L	
Willet	*Catoptrophorus semipalmatus*	4	4	4	4	BL	
Spotted Sandpiper	*Actitis macularia*	2	2	2		L	?
Whimbrel	*Numenius phaeopus*	4	2	2	2	BL	
Long-billed Curlew	*Numenius americanus*	3	1	1	2	L	
Marbled Godwit	*Limosa fedoa*	4	3	3	4	BL	
Ruddy Turnstone	*Arenaria interpres*	1		1		BL	
Black Turnstone	*Arenaria melanocephala*	1		1		BL	
Red Knot	*Calidris canutus*	1				L	
Sanderling	*Calidris alba*	4	5	4		B	
Western Sandpiper	*Calidris mauri*	3	3	3	1	L	
Least Sandpiper	*Calidris minutilla*	3	3	3	1	L	
Baird's Sandpiper	*Calidris bairdii*	1				L	
Dunlin	*Calidris alpina*	2	1	1		L	
Stilt Sandpiper	*Calidris himantopus*	1				L	
Short-billed Dowitcher	*Limnodromus griseus*	2	2	2		L	
Long-billed Dowitcher	*Limnodromus scolopaceus*	2	2	2		L	
Common Snipe	*Gallinago gallinago*		1			L	
Red-necked Phalarope	*Phalaropus lobatus*	1				L	
LARIDAE - GULLS AND TERNS							
Parasitic Jaeger	*Stercorarius parasiticus*	1	1	1		O	
Bonaparte's Gull	*Larus philadelphia*		2	1		OBL	
Heermann's Gull	*Larus heermanni*	5	5	2	4	OBL	
Mew Gull	*Larus canus*		2	1		OBL	
Ring-billed Gull	*Larus delawarensis*	4	5	4	3	OBL	
California Gull	*Larus californicus*	4	5	4	2	OBL	
Herring Gull	*Larus argentatus*		2	2		OBL	
Thayer's Gull	*Larus thayeri*		1	1		OBL	
Western Gull	*Larus occidentalis*	5	5	5	5	OBL	
Glaucous-winged Gull	*Larus glaucescens*	2	2	2		OBL	
Caspian Tern	*Sterna caspia*	3	3	3	4	OL	
Royal Tern	*Sterna maxima*	3	2	3	2	OL	
Elegant Tern	*Sterna elegans*	2		4	3	OL	
Common Tern	*Sterna hirundo*	2				OL	
Forster's Tern	*Sterna forsteri*	3	4	4	4	OL	
Least Tern	*Sterna antillarum*			2	2	OL	+#
Black Skimmer	*Rynchops niger*				1	OL	
COLUMBIDAE - PIGEONS AND DOVES							
Rock Dove	*Columba livia*	3	3	3	3	L	*
Mourning Dove	*Zenaida macroura*	3	4	4	3	WC	*
TYTONIDAE - BARN OWLS							
Common Barn-Owl	*Tyto alba*	1	1	1	1	WP	?
STRIGIDAE - TYPICAL OWLS							
Great Horned Owl	*Bubo virginianus*	1	1	1	1	WP	?

105

Common Name	Scientific Name	Seasonal Abundance				Habitats	Status
		F	W	S	Su		
APODIDAE - SWIFTS							
Vaux's Swift	*Chaetura vauxi*			1		LCP	
White-throated Swift	*Aeronautes saxatalis*	2	2	3	2	P	*
TROCHILIDAE - HUMMINGBIRDS							
Black-chinned Hummingbird	*Archilochus alexandri*			1	1	WCP	
Anna's Hummingbird	*Calypte anna*	4	4	4	4	WCP	*
Costa's Hummingbird	*Calypte costae*			2	1	WCP	*
Calliope Hummingbird	*Stellula calliope*			1	1	WCP	
Rufous Hummingbird	*Selasphorus rufus*			1	1	WCP	
Allen's Hummingbird	*Selasphorus sasin*			1	1	WCP	
ALCEDINIDAE - KINGFISHERS							
Belted Kingfisher	*Ceryle alcyon*	3	3	2	2	L	
PICIDAE - WOODPECKERS							
Acorn Woodpecker	*Melanerpes formicivorus*	1				P	
Nuttall's Woodpecker	*Picoides nuttallii*	3	3	3	3	WP	
Downy Woodpecker	*Picoides pubescens*	1	1	1	1	WP	
Northern Flicker	*Colaptes auratus*	3	3	3	3	WP	*
TYRANNIDAE - TYRANT FLYCATCHERS							
Olive-sided Flycatcher	*Contopus borealis*			1		P	
Western Wood-Pewee	*Contopus sordidulus*	1		1		WP	
Willow Flycatcher	*Empidonax traillii*			1		W	
Hammond's Flycatcher	*Empidonax hammondii*			1		WP	
Pacific-slope Flycatcher	*Empidonax difficilis*	1		2		WP	*
Black Phoebe	*Sayornis nigricans*	3	4	3	2	LCP	*
Say's Phoebe	*Sayornis saya*	2	3	2		LC	
Ash-throated Flycatcher	*Myiarchus cinerascens*			3	3	WC	*
Tropical Kingbird	*Tyrannus melancholicus*	1				CP	
Cassin's Kingbird	*Tyrannus vociferans*	2	2	2	2	CP	
Western Kingbird	*Tyrannus verticalis*			2	2	CP	
ALAUDIDAE - LARKS							
Horned Lark	*Eremophila alpestris*	1				L	
HIRUNDINIDAE - SWALLOWS							
Tree Swallow	*Tachycineta bicolor*		2	2		LCP	
Violet-green Swallow	*Tachycineta thalassina*			1	1	LCP	
Rough-winged Swallow	*Stelgidopteryx serripennis*			3	3	LCP	*
Cliff Swallow	*Hirundo lunifrons*	2		3	5	LCP	*
Barn Swallow	*Hirundo rustica*	2		2	1	LCP	
CORVIDAE - JAYS, MAGPIES, AND CROWS							
Scrub Jay	*Aphelocoma coerulescens*	4	4	4	4	WCP	*
American Crow	*Corvus brachyrhynchos*		1	1		LCP	
Common Raven	*Corvus corax*	4	4	4	4	LCP	*
AEGITHALIDAE - BUSHTIT							
Bushtit	*Psaltriparus minimus*	4	4	4	4	WCP	*
TROGLODYTIDAE - WRENS							
Rock Wren	*Salpinctes obsoletus*	1				C	
Bewick's Wren	*Troglodytes bewickii*	4	4	4	4	WCP	*
House Wren	*Troglodytes aedon*	4	3	4	3	WCP	*
Marsh Wren	*Cistothorus palustris*	3	3	3	3	L	*

106

Common Name	Scientific Name	Seasonal Abundance F	W	S	Su	Habitats	Status
MUSCICAPIDAE - GNATCATCHERS, KINGLETS, THRUSHES, BLUEBIRDS, WRENTIT)							
Ruby-crowned Kinglet	Regulus calendula	3	3	3		WCP	
Blue-gray Gnatcatcher	Polioptila caerulea	2		2		WC	
California Gnatcatcher	Polioptila californica	3	3	3	3	C	*#
Western Bluebird	Sialia mexicana	12/2/90					
Swainson's Thrush	Catharus ustulatus	1		1		WCP	*
Hermit Thrush	Catharus guttatus	2	3	3		WCP	
American Robin	Turdus migratorius	2	2	2		P	
Wrentit	Chamaea fasciata	4	4	4	4	CP	*
MIMIDAE - MOCKINGBIRDS AND THRASHERS							
Northern Mockingbird	Mimus polyglottos	3	3	3	3	P	*
California Thrasher	Toxostoma redivivum	4	4	4	4	CP	*
MOTACILLIDAE - WAGTAILS AND PIPITS							
American Pipit	Anthus rubescens	1	1			L	
BOMBYCILLIDAE - WAXWINGS							
Cedar Waxwing	Bombycilla cedrorum	2	2	2		CP	
PTILOGONATIDAE - SILKY FLYCATCHERS							
Phainopepla	Phainopepla nitens	1				CP	
LANIIDAE - SHRIKES							
Loggerhead Shrike	Lanius ludovicianus	2	2	1	2	LCP	?
STURNIDAE - STARLINGS							
European Starling	Sturnus vulgaris	3	3	3	3	LW	*
VIREONIDAE - TYPICAL VIREOS							
Bell's Vireo	Vireo bellii			1		W	?#
Solitary Vireo	Vireo solitarius			1		WP	
Hutton's Vireo	Vireo huttoni	1	1	1		WP	
Warbling Vireo	Vireo gilvus	1		1		WP	
EMBERIZIDAE - WARBLERS, SPARROWS, BLACKBIRDS AND RELATIVES							
Orange-crowned Warbler	Vermivora celata	1	1	3	2	WP	*
Nashville Warbler	Vermivora ruficapilla			1		WP	
Yellow Warbler	Dendroica petechia	1		1	1	WP	*
Yellow-rumped Warbler	Dendroica coronata	4	4	4		WCP	
Black-throated Gray Warbler	Dendroica nigrescens			1		WP	
Townsend's Warbler	Dendroica townsendi	1		1		WP	
Hermit Warbler	Dendroica occidentalis			1		WP	
American Redstart	Setophaga ruticilla	1				W	
MacGillivray's Warbler	Oporornis tolmiei			1		W	
Common Yellowthroat	Geothlypis trichas	4	4	4	4	LW	*
Wilson's Warbler	Wilsonia pusilla			2		WCP	
Yellow-breasted Chat	Icteria virens	1		1		W	*

107

Common Name	Scientific Name	F	W	S	Su	Habitats	Status
EMBERIZIDAE - WARBLERS, SPARROWS, BLACKBIRDS AND RELATIVES (CONTINUED)							
Western Tanager	*Piranga ludoviciana*	1		2		WP	
Black-headed Grosbeak	*Pheucticus melanocephalus*			2	2	WP	*
Blue Grosbeak	*Guiraca caerulea*			2		W	*
Lazuli Bunting	*Passerina amoena*	1				WC	
Rufous-sided Towhee	*Pipilo erythrophtalmus*	3	3	3	3	WCP	*
California Towhee	*Pipilo crissalis*	4	4	4	4	CP	*
Rufous-crowned Sparrow	*Aimophila ruficeps*	3	3	3	3	C	*
Chipping Sparrow	*Spizella passerina*	1	1			C	
Lark Sparrow	*Chondestes grammacus*	1				C	
Savannah Sparrow	*Passerculus sandwichensis*						
migrants	*P. s. sps.*	2	3	2		LC	
Belding's	*P. s. beldingii*	4	4	4	4	BL	*#
Large-billed	*P. s. rostratus*	1	1			BL	
Fox Sparrow	*Zonotrichia iliaca*	2	2			C	
Song Sparrow	*Zonotrichia melodia*	5	5	5	5	WC	*
Lincoln's Sparrow	*Zonotrichia lincolnii*		2	2		WC	
Golden-crowned Sparrow	*Zonotrichia atricapilla*	2	2	2		WCP	
White-crowned Sparrow	*Zonotrichia leucophrys*	3	3	4		WCP	
Dark-eyed Junco	*Junco hyemalis*	2		1		CP	
Red-winged Blackbird	*Agelaius phoeniceus*	4	4	4	4	LWC	*
Western Meadowlark	*Sturnella neglecta*	3	3	3	2	C	*
Brewer's Blackbird	*Euphagus cyanocephalus*	4	4	4	4	LC	*
Brown-headed Cowbird	*Molothrus ater*			1	1	LWC	*
Hooded Oriole	*Icterus cucullatus*			1	1	WCP	
Northern Oriole	*Icterus galbula*			2	1	WCP	*
FRINGILLIDAE - FINCHES							
Purple Finch	*Carpodacus purpureus*	1		1		WCP	
House Finch	*Carpodacus mexicanus*	5	5	5	5	WCP	*
Pine Siskin	*Carduelis pinus*	1		1		P	
Lesser Goldfinch	*Carduelis psaltria*	3	3	3	3	WCP	*
Lawrence's Goldfinch	*Carduelis lawrencei*	1				WCP	
American Goldfinch	*Carduelis tristis*	2	2	2	2	WCP	*
PASSERIDAE - WEAVER FINCHES							
House Sparrow	*Passer domesticus*	2	2	2	2	L	*

Note: Extirpated and very rare birds omitted.